Y0-BRC-109

# Reader's Comments

*. . . Arnold Bocksel, survivor of three and a half years of cruel impri-sonment, recalls exact details of the events that occurred almost a half century ago in a most remarkable, interesting and believable manner . . .*

*. . . readers are often not certain whether they are being told of events that happened to the author during World War II, or now. Perhaps, for the author there is little difference . . .*

*. . . true epic with deep emotional impact of the horrors experienced in Japanese prison camps . . .*

*. . .powerful & emotional depiction. Proof that freedom is never free. . .*

*. . . well written and factual . . .*

*. . . I have despaired for you and laughed with you; felt the depths of your depressions and the highs of your hopes. A powerful recording of an event about which I knew nothing . . .*

*. . . true life drama of Americans as Japanese prisoners of war. . .*

*. . . incredible story, almost unbelievable . . .*

# RICE · MEN AND BARBED WIRE

*by Arnold A. Bocksel*

**Published by:**
**Michael B. Glass & Associates**
**Hempstead, New York**

# Acknowledgements

*Very special thanks to . . .*

. . . *Louis Panagini, Artist,*
   *who with great insight and perception*
   *inspired the design of the cover.*


. . . *Annedorle Sreckovich, Able Manuscript Service*
   *in Douglaston, New York, for her dedication*
   *and expertise in editing and word*
   *processing the manuscript.*


. . . *Michael B. Glass & Associates, Inc.,*
   *Graphic Design Printing & Publishing Organization*
   *of Hempstead, New York, and the entire staff of that*
   *company for working with me, offering helpful suggestions*
   *and ideas and manufacturing and printing "Rice Men*
   *and Barbed Wire" in their own studio from the*
   *original typewritten manuscript and collection*
   *of photographs that I first brought to them.*


**A.A.B.**

# Contents

1. The Beginning
2. Fighting on Bataan & Corregidor
3. Women Warriors
4. Fall of Corregidor
5. Capture
6. Bibibid Prison
7. Box Car Journey
8. Cabanatuan Prison Camp
9. Decapitation
10. Sickness & Diseases
11. Cabanatuan Prison Camp
12. "Hell Ships"
13. Voyage to Manchuria
14. POW's in Manchuria
15. Mukden, Manchuria Prison Camp
16. Profile, Dan
17. Life in Mukden
18. Corporal Noda, "The Rat"
19. Vagaries
20. Time Passes in Mukden
21. POW Buddies
22. Chicken Saga
23. Red Cross Packages
24. General McArthur Steps Ashore at Leyte
25. "Hell Ships" Journeys
26. Bombing of a Prison Camp
27. Religious Solace
28. Musings
29. Christmas Under the Red Sun
30. Lt. Hegecata, Benefactor
31. "White Rats" in Prison Camp
32. Samples of Japanese Art
33. Vera Brittain Extracts
34. Women and Prison Life
35. Mukden Prison Camp -1945
36. Liberation by Russians
37. Post Liberation
38. USNS Hospital Ship RELIEF
39. Okinawa Visit
40. Manila & Journey to San Francisco
41. Family Reunion
42. Atomic Bomb & Thoughts
43. Comments About Japanese
44. Concluding

*Dedicated to all those men*
*who shared these experiences;*
*Especially those who did not return,*
*those who gave up their tomorrows*
*so we could have our todays.*

## ALONG THE ROAD

*I walked a mile with Pleasure*
*She chattered all the way;*
*But left me none the wiser,*
*For all she had to say.*

*I walked a mile with Sorrow*
*And ne'er a word said she;*
*But, oh the things I learned from her*
*When Sorrow walked with me.*

*Robert Browning Hamilton*

II

## PREFACE

Many times throughout history, in past wars, captors have ill-treated and often killed their prisoners. History abounds in these "horror stories." In the United States itself, cruelty and atrocities were perpetrated on prisoners of war during the Civil War. The inhuman treatment meted out to the Union prisoners of war by the Confederacy is documented in history and stands high in the annals of crimes committed against helpless human beings.

The infamous Confederate Prisoner of War Camp located at Andersonville, Georgia, will always remain a dark, dimly lit beacon of man's inhumanity to man. Approximately 50,000 Union soldiers suffered under the savagery of a cruel camp commandant, and 14,000 perished due to the unrelenting cruelty imposed upon them. A statistic leaving a permanent stain on the honor of the Confederacy.

(In fairness, I must also state that the North also had some terrible prison camps in which the Rebels were incarcerated. They suffered and died there too, however not anywhere near the magnitude of Andersonville.)

The Nazi Holocaust, in which 6,000,000 men, women, and children were murdered, will forever be among the greatest crimes committed against mankind. The depths of degradation the Nazi's stooped to in this carnage will forever remain a monument to man's evil and hatred. Love, kindness, and compassion were censored words in their vocabulary and in their hearts. Their evil, and the depths it descended to, will forever be recorded in the history of man's evil. Their bloody stains can never be erased. Ugly wounds heal, but the scars always remain as a living reminder.

In World War II the Japanese became members of this "elite" group. They, too, wrote many pages in the history books of evil and hatred with their cruel, sadistic, and inhuman treatment of prisoners of war whom they captured during World War II. Americans, Filipinos, British, Dutch, and Australian prisoners of war were subjected to their unjust and fanatical hatred. Few survived their incarceration. Of the American forces alone, approximately 25,000 were prisoners and only 9,700 survived. Other captured nationalities suffered, at least, the same casualty ratios.

The Japanese have written shameful pages in history before World War II. In the *Rape of Nanking*, 340,000 men, women and children were reportedly slaughtered, and in Manchuria they added more pages to the history books with their policy of kill, loot, and burn. At Ping-Ding Shan they reportedly massacred 3,000 men, women and children by machine gunning them to death. Millions were forced into Japanese labor camps. What the Japanese call the *"China Incident"* resulted in the deaths of millions of Chinese. A classic example of barbarism in the 20th century.

The American Defenders of Bataan and Corregidor became the first forces in our Nation's history to surrender to an enemy. Lack of food, ammunition, medicines, a hopeless situation with no prospects of relief or help coming from the U.S.; and a numerically vastly superior enemy force were the basic circumstances that dictated surrender.

Endurance and hope had slowly expired under the strains suffered by the defenders. There was no alternative.

Surrendered, but not in fear or shame.

The pages following are a story of the Japanese of World War II as conquerors and captors, inflicting and venting their fanatical hatred and cruelty on a group of honorable, weak, sick and exhausted men. It is a story of man's inhumanity to man, Japanese *"Bushido"* style.

The factual statements in the text are documented. My statements are a reflection of my personal thoughts, feelings, and views of this experience.

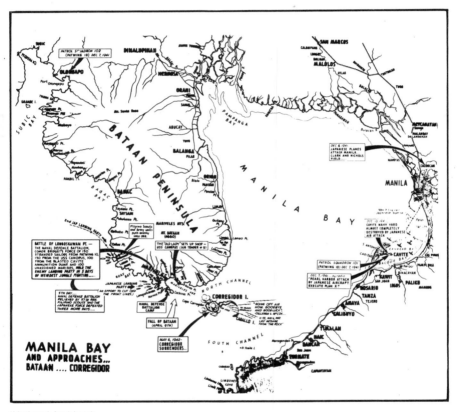

(National Archives)

V

*1*

It was late May, 1942, when we arrived at a small
railroad station some 10 miles outside of Manila, in the
Philippines. It was a dreary day, the station was filthy, and
not a "redcap" in sight to handle baggage. There was no
train announcer either. Instead, you received personal
directions to your "reserved space"...in one of the boxcars.

A rifle butt in the ass meant *"move it";* one in the
face meant *"you are not moving fast enough";* and a bayonet
in the stomach meant *"so sorry Joe, you just missed the train."*

We were American prisoners of war, remnants of the
Defenders of Bataan and Corregidor, enrolled in the
freshman class of prisoner of war school, with a complete
Japanese faculty. We learned a lot from our Japanese
instructors before we matriculated, some three and one half
years later. The "drop out" rate was alarmingly high, too.

Before we start classes, I would like to take you back
to the beginning.

\* \* \* \* \* \* \* \*

It has been said that when the band stops playing, the
war is over. This story is recounted while the band was still
playing, as I boarded the *S.S. President Coolidge* bound for
Manila, Philippines. I am 27 years of age, happy and care-
free, enroute for two years of service in the Philippines,
having volunteered for the U.S. Army along with my
younger brother Raymond, some few months previously. I

have been assigned as Chief Engineer of the U.S. Army Mine Planter *Harrison,* with the rank of Chief Warrant Officer-4. The *Harrison* was stationed at Corregidor in Manila Bay, off the Bataan Peninsula, under command of the Harbor Defenses of Manila & Subic Bays.

The ship's lines are let go, the whistle blasts several times, tug boats ease the vessels out into San Francisco Bay, and we soon pass under the Golden Gate Bridge. The band is still playing loudly.

I am travelling with the 200th Coast Artillery from New Mexico who have been assigned to the defense of the Philippines. They are a National Guard Unit that has been activated for this duty. Luckily, I am berthed in one of the passenger cabins along with another officer, Jim McCahon. I made many friends among them, especially Dan McCartney and Al Wheeler, who shared closely in the POW experience with me.

We arrived in Manila in late September 1941 and I reported aboard the mine planter at Corregidor. Corregidor is a small rocky island, shaped like a tadpole, and situated in the South China Sea at the entrance to Manila Bay. It was the *"Gibraltar"* of the Philippines, protecting the entrances to Manila Bay.

Manila was a gay, beautiful city, called the Pearl of the Orient, and located on the Island of Luzon, one of over 7,000 islands in the Archipelago. I tasted the delights she had to offer with great gusto and was introduced to all the favorite haunts by several of my companions in the mine planter service. I found the Filipina women warm, friendly, and gracious. As I remember, I fell in love practically every weekend during those early days in Manila, when a siren was a beautiful woman and not an air raid alarm, as we later learned. Our uniforms at that time were white coats, black trousers, and black shoes. I loved the bar and cocktail lounge at the Manila Hotel, especially the Fiesta Pavilion, where I spent many happy moments. With Scotch Whiskey

2

Author left, with his brother Raymond at Submarine Mine Depot School, Ft. Monroe. July 1941

Author at time of his departure for the Philippines. Sept. 1941

at about 30 cents a drink, free hors d'oeuvres, and lovely music, how could you miss? I remember one hors d'oeuvre that was made of anchovies fried in bananas. Delicious! We also had great fun at the Jai Lai Club, Military Clubs, and other cocktail lounges around town. Could have used some air conditioners at times, even though the ceilings were covered with fans, slowly blowing the air downwards. It was a fun time, and I can still hear the clinking of ice in frosty glasses, remember the smells of the flowers; the fun filled atmosphere complete with laughter and the heady smells of youth; the strains of the orchestra playing softly the beautiful and meaningful music of the '40s; and just about everything else that was meant for youth to splurge with.

There was a lot of war talk in those days, but not one of us seriously believed that the Japanese would actually attack us. An article in *LIFE* Magazine in November 1941 predicted that in the event of war with the Japanese they would be defeated in two weeks time, by the Navy alone. The article further stated that the Japs could not bomb accurately due to genetically poor vision and inferior quality aircraft; that they were slovenly and ill-disciplined, and that their warships were poorly designed, etc. Someone must have had a "red face" on December 7, 1941! The Japanese turned out to be well-trained, fearless, rigidly disciplined, with splendid military hardware, and a spiritual quality to their militarism related to the deity like figure of their Emperor. They were tough bastards.

When the Japs came over to the Philippines on December 8, 1941, they gave us a licking almost like the one they inflicted on Pearl Harbor. Our planes were caught on the ground at Clark and Nichols Field (many had been up in the air but had come in for refueling). In the first day they decimated our Air Force in the Philippines. A few planes survived, but they were only a token force. Then they hit our naval base at Cavite in Manila Bay, pummeling

3

it practically out of use. Many naval vessels escaped destruction primarily because they were out at sea, away from the base. In essence, we had no Air Force and a severely wounded Navy in the Philippines. Bad eyesight? Inferior aircraft? The Jap "Zeros" were probably the most advanced and superior military aircraft of the times.

I suspect that even if our Air Force had survived in the Philippines, it could not have maintained its effectiveness against the numerical superiority of the Japanese Air Forces.

The crippling of our Naval forces at Pearl Harbor prevented our sea lanes from being open and eliminated the viable possibility of supplying arms, munitions, and reinforcements to the beleaguered forces on Bataan and Corregidor. This lack of U.S. Naval support enabled the enemy to effectively blockade the Philippines. The debacle at Pearl Harbor contributed immensely to the doom of our potential air power in the Philippines, and doomed the defenders of Bataan and Corregidor, especially so as the wartime policy was to concentrate primarily on the defeat of Germany and Japan secondly, sealing our fates.

We were expendable.

The astonishing success of the Japanese at Pearl Harbor can only be attributed to the massive "Intelligence Disaster" we experienced at that time. History indicates that we had broken the Japanese secret codes and were aware that an attack was imminent. This information was apparently not timely transmitted to the commands at Hawaii and the Philippines. A monumental, sad, and costly blunder for the United States.

*2*

How in the hell we lasted until April 9, 1942 on Bataan, and May 6, 1942 on Corregidor, is beyond belief. It can only be attributed to the grim determination of our forces, aided by the almost impassable terrain of the jungles of Bataan which were of enormous significance in impeding the advance of the Japanese. Other factors contributing to the capitulation of our forces were hunger, rampant sickness (primarily malaria and dengue fever), lack of ammunition, and the hopelessness of the situation. In March of 1942 most of us realized that no help would be forthcoming from the United States. Someone said it better than I:

> *Men fighting with an unshakable faith are made of something more than flesh, but they are not made of steel. The flesh must yield at last; endurance must melt away, and the end must come. But through the bloody haze of the last reverberating shot there shall always remain the vision of grim, gaunt men, still unafraid.*

The Bataan-Corregidor mission was accomplished. We had been fighting a delaying action and upsetting the Jap timetable for further quick conquests in the Pacific; additionally, this allowed the U.S. more time to recoup and rebuild some of the heavy losses sustained at the onset of the war.

It is noteworthy to point out that all of our

equipment in the Philippines was of WWI vintage, including the level brim steel helmets, which primarily had great use as a wash basin.

Obviously, our War Plans dictated that the forces fighting in the Philippines were expendable. News Correspondent Frank Hewlett wrote:

*We're the Battling Bastards of Bataan,*
*No Mama, no Papa, no Uncle Sam,*
*No Aunts, no Cousins, no Uncles, no Nieces*
*No pills, no planes, no artillery pieces*
*And nobody gives a damn.*

The *New York Times* wrote:

*Bataan has been lost but it will be remembered generations from now.   The delaying actions performed will take their place in the annals of American History.*

The *Washington Times* wrote:

*Tributes of words seem empty and inadequate. It is enough to say the Defenders of Bataan will be immortal.*

Prior to our capture, we on the mine planter were still laying and maintaining mines in the mine fields protecting the entrance to Manila and Subic Bays as well as the lower Bataan Peninsula.  In the latter months of the war, most of our missions were carried out at night when we had some respite from the constant shelling from the Jap batteries on the Bataan Peninsula as well as the continual aerial bombardments experienced during the daylight hours.

The Army Mine Planter Service was a branch of the

6

Coast Artillery Corps. The mines, called "submarine mines," were planted in the sea in exact locations and charted; offering protection against enemy shipping and submarines. Each mine contained a charge of approximately 2,000 lbs of TNT and was lowered to rest on the ocean floor. The planting, maintaining, and recovery of the mines was the function of the Army Mine Planter Service and required the most precise handling of the vessel in order to effect these services. Each individual mine was connected to cables, so control of the mines was effected through the shore Mine Battery. The weight of the mine was sufficient to hold it in position on the ocean floor. The mines were planted several hundred feet apart and could be fired singly or as a group. The mines were so connected that they also could give warning of any approaching submarine or surface vessel; they could be fired manually to destroy a vessel passing over the mine; and they could be set to automatically detonate due to the impact of the magnetic field of a passing vessel on the mine. Optional decisions on the mine settings were determined by the Mine Command Post on shore. The mine planter was a vessel of approximately 170 feet in length with a 32 foot beam, and powered by two steam reciprocating engines for maximum maneuverability. The usual ship complement was 8-9 officers and about 40 enlisted personnel. Two fifty caliber machine guns were mounted on the vessel as its only armor.

Not a single enemy vessel was ever successful in passing through the mine fields in the Philippines. During enemy air raids and shellings, the mine planter was forced to continue any mine laying operation they were involved in at the time as the mines could not be cut loose.

At this time, fuel oil was running low for the mine planter as well as several small naval vessels operating in this area. I suggested to our commanding officer, Captain E. Rosenstock, that there was a strong possibility that we might locate fuel oil on some of the many sunken American

7

and Filipino vessels in Manila Bay. The main problem was that these vessels lay sunken in close proximity to the newly established Jap lines on the Bataan Peninsula.

Four of the mine planter personnel, Captain Rosenstock, Sgt. Dee, Cpl. Creasanzo, and myself accomplished the mission in a small motor launch. We searched through the sunken vessels for fuel oil, sounding the double bottom tanks where fuel is generally stored. We found oil on two of the vessels. We were subjected to severe enemy fire from the enemy now located on the shores of Bataan, but luckily returned to the mine planter unscathed. The discovery of oil was transmitted to the Navy and they recovered much of the oil under cover of darkness. Enough oil was salvaged to refuel all the remaining vessels in the area.

Some weeks later, the mine planter was attacked by Jap dive bombers. Two of them, with blazing red sun insignias (we called them "flaming assholes") swooped down and got hits on the mine planter. The two 50 caliber machine guns we had as our only protection were obviously not very effective. The vessel was severely damaged and rendered inoperable. Four of our crew were killed in this attack, James Murray, Skipper; Eugene Walz, Engineer; and two crew members. The surviving crew members, including myself, were assigned to the defense of Corregidor. Corregidor fell about one month later, capitulating on May 6, 1942.

About a month previous to the fall of Corregidor, the mine planter was in Marivelles on the Bataan Peninsula, the day that Bataan surrendered. That evening was a nightmare I can never forget. The sky was lit up like a gigantic 4th of July celebration. Artillery shells screaming through the air, ammunition dumps being blown up, continuous gun fire, tremendous detonations, hot sticky air resounding with explosive charges, men leaping into the bay to escape; chaos and havoc all around. We picked up survivors from the beaches, from the water, and any other place we found them and returned to Corregidor with the survivors. These men escaped only to endure the same experience a month later on Corregidor. From the frying pan into the fire. If we were brave, I know we were fearful too. However, fear passes but always leaves a record of its stay.

I recalled McArthur's message to us in January 1942:

*Help is on the way; thousands of troops and hundreds of planes are being dispatched. The exact time of arrival of reinforcements is unknown as they will have to fight their way through Japanese attempts against them. It is imperative that our troops hold until these reinforcements arrive. No further retreat is possible. We have more troops in Bataan than the Japanese have thrown against us; our supplies are ample; a determined defense will defeat the enemy's attack. It is a question now of courage and determination. Men who run will merely be destroyed, but men who fight will save themselves and their country. I call upon every soldier in Bataan to fight in his assigned position resisting every attack. This is the only road to salvation. If we fight we will win; if we retreat, we shall be destroyed.*

There is no question that at that time General McArthur believed that help was on the way and that our forces were not expendable.

During these times we were constantly receiving "invitations" from the Japs to surrender. Passes to surrender; reminders that we were doomed; that our wives and girlfriends were sleeping with other men; and on and on. We only got a laugh out of them.

During the five months of warfare in the Philippines, Corregidor was subjected to 384 aerial bombardments and

9

constant shelling from April 6th to May 6th after the Japs fully occupied the Bataan Peninsula. On May 4th alone, it was recorded that 16,000 artillery shells fell on Corregidor. I was caught in one very severe shelling one night that I can't ever forget. Shell after shell exploded around us in a world changed to lights, flames, explosions and screams. Between the shell bursts you could hear the cries of the wounded and dying. When the shelling eventually stopped, the area looked like an outdoor butcher shop. Legs dangling from trees and boulders, a loose arm here and there, other pieces of bodies scattered all around; a mouth frozen open in amazement; another with teeth grimly clenched; a skull that looked like a burst open ripened tomato with insides scattered and bloody; two men with their arms around each other frozen in death; men dying, gurgling, frothing blood spewing from their mouths, gasping for breath.

Shouts of *"Medic, Medic"* filled the air. You think they should be calling for "garbage disposal," and tears fill your eyes as you try to help in the carnage.

The sound of those shells and the cries of those men will forever be etched in my memory. No, we can't glorify war, but we can glorify those men who served, especially those who made the supreme sacrifice.

This part of war does not evoke memories of marching bands and militaristic music. It deals only with death.

*3*

At this point I would be remiss if I did not pay recognition and tribute to those gallant women who served alongside us: The Army and Navy nurses. These women shared all of the dangers and deprivations that the fighting men of Bataan and Corregidor endured. They were the fighting women of Bataan and Corregidor. They served selflessly in the makeshift hospitals on the battlefield, performing their ministrations to the sick and wounded during air raids, shellings, and while the fighting went on around them. They went for days and days with no rest, serving, serving.

Sixty-eight were captured by the Japanese and imprisoned for almost three years in the Philippines. Twenty-two of the other nurses escaped just a few days prior to the surrender of the Philippines, some by air, others by submarine. One planeload of nurses made it to Australia; the other was forced to land shortly after take-off. The nurses on the submarine *Spearfish* made it safely to Australia after 17 days underwater. I brought several of the nurses to the debarkation area where the submarine was rendezvousing in the sea off Corregidor.

Lieutenants Helen Summers, Lucy Wilson, and Ann Bernatitus were among those nurses whom I still remember escaping on the submarine. Helen visited my family after she returned to the States in June 1942 and my folks said it was like receiving a message from heaven, delivered by an angel. We maintained our friendship after the war until her

11

early death in the '60s. Almost all of the nurses who escaped continued to serve in the military after they were returned to the U.S.

Ann Bernatitus served again as a navy nurse and was the chief nurse on the U.S. Navy Hospital ship *Relief* when it evacuated those American prisoners of war liberated at war's end in Korea and Manchuria. I was among them.

Lucy Wilson returned to the Pacific Theater as a flight nurse and was assigned to an air evacuation unit flying into hostile enemy territory evacuating the sick and wounded. Her unit flew out the first American prisoners of war liberated by the American forces in the Philippines.

Jean Kennedy, one of the incarcerated nurses, kept my college ring for me throughout the war and after her liberation sent the ring home to my mother, some 7-8 months prior to my liberation.

Gwen Henshaw, another incarcerated nurse, did the same with my personal papers which I had entrusted to her, and found waiting for me when I was liberated.

General Wainwright gave these nurses the name of "Angels of Bataan," a beautiful and justly earned tribute which these gallant women so richly deserved. We salute them proudly and forever.

A not so well known statistic is that over 200 American women in the Armed Forces were killed in WWII.

HEADQUARTERS 13TH AIR FORCE, Southwest Pacific.—Lucy Wilson, the pretty Big Sandy, Texas, girl who was the last Army nurse to leave Corregidor, has won another decoration for "courage and devotion to duty."

Still in the Pacific combat zone, Lucy, now a captain in the 13th Air Force's air evacuation outfit, was awarded the Air Medal for making numerous flights into hostile territory to bring out sick and wounded soldiers.

Lucy Wilson Jopling, one of the "Angels of Bataan".

*4*

The defenses of Corregidor were primarily planned against sea invasion, but the Japs didn't come in that way because from the sea, Corregidor was almost impregnable. When they took possession of the Bataan Peninsula, their guns pummeled Corregidor day and night. Our gun placements were not as effective as planned. We all knew the end was in sight and that no aid was forthcoming from the U.S., especially after the fall of Bataan. Reinforcements would never reach us in time. General Edward King, the Commander of troops on Bataan, realized this when contrary to orders he surrendered his sick, hungry, and worn out forces to avoid the further useless shedding of blood. It was among the bravest feats a general has ever had to perform.

Speaking about generals, I would like to say a few words about General Douglas McArthur. I admired him enormously. Some men didn't, but that's the way it is with all generals. Among the myths about him was the one that referred to him as "Dugout Doug," the inference being that he would jump into a dugout or foxhole during bombings and shellings. I even hate to dignify this scurrilous myth by repeating it; however I must refute it because of my own experience in this regard. One day on Corregidor I was caught in a very severe artillery barrage. Standing only a few feet away from me was General McArthur. Everyone in the vicinity, including me, hit the dirt, fast and hard...that is, except McArthur. He never moved, flinched, ducked, or wavered during the intense shelling. He stood ramrod straight, no helmet on, smoking his corn cob pipe, and he never missed a puff. If he was selling morale that day, he did one hell of a job, but you know what I felt...that he wasn't one goddamned bit frightened. When it was over, he smiled and waved at us. I don't think he knew the meaning of fear.

On the fall of Bataan he said,

> *The Bataan force went out as it would have wished, fighting to the end its flickering, forlorn hope. No Army has done so much with so little, and nothing became it more than its last moment of trial and agony. To the weeping mothers of its dead, I can only say that the sacrifice and halo of Jesus of Nazareth has descended upon their sons, and that God will take them unto Himself.*

Many other apocryphal stories have been related concerning McArthur, but they are all rubbish. He was among the greatest generals our nation has known and deserving of our deepest respect and admiration. His brilliance, both as a warrior and statesman, coupled with his compassion and kindness, are abundantly documented in history. When he returned to the Philippines and visited his former troops in the POW barracks, he broke down and cried...and reportedly said, *"I'm sorry it took so long."* He cared.

General, you once said that old soldiers just fade away. Sorry, Sir, you are wrong, you will never fade away.

So long as we are on the subject of generals, I would be remiss if I didn't comment about the last general I served under. General Jonathan Wainwright. I start with the message he sent to President Roosevelt on the surrender of

Corregidor, about a month after the fall of Bataan:

*With broken heart and head bowed in sadness, but not in shame, I report to your excellency that today I must arrange terms for the surrender of the fortified islands of Manila Bay. There is a limit of human endurance, and that limit has long since passed. Without prospect of relief, I feel it is my duty to my country and my gallant men to end this useless effusion of blood and human sacrifice.*

*If you agree, Mr. President, please say to the nation that my troops and I have accomplished all that is humanely possible and that we have upheld the best traditions of the United States and its Armies.*

*May God bless and preserve you, and guide you and the nation in the effort to ultimate victory.*

*With profound regret and with continued pride in my gallant troops I go to meet the Japanese commander. Goodbye, Mr. President.*

This message reflects the greatness of this general under whom I am proud to have served. He earned and was deserving of every star he wore...each one not only shining with his bravery and brilliance but also with great love and compassion for his men. He was affectionately called "Skinny Wainwright." I don't know if it was because he was thin or because he came from Skaneateles, N.Y.

The surrender action was obviously dictated by the facts that we could no longer hold out against the Japs because we were greatly outnumbered; incessant aerial bombardments and continual shelling, over which we had no defense; failing food and medical supplies; lack of ammunition; the remaining garrison consisting of a small group of sick, tired, and gaunt men with no hope of reinforcements coming from the U.S.

The enemy was contacted and General Wainwright, under a flag of truce, crossed Manila Bay to meet with the Japanese commander, General Homma. Wainwright's offer to surrender Corregidor was furiously rejected by Homma, unless Wainwright also surrendered all other units in the Philippines engaged against the Japanese (Wainwright stated that he had no control over the other units fighting elsewhere in the Philippines).

He returned to Corregidor with the renewed threat by Homma to resume fighting unless there was immediate surrender of all forces. In anticipation of surrender, the forces there were ordered to destroy their guns and ammunition.

On Corregidor, Wainwright made the agonizing decision to surrender the complete archipelago of the Philippines. The next day he was taken to Manila and made to broadcast surrender messages to the commanders of the remaining U.S. forces in other locations in the Philippines.

We have become prisoners of war, or so we thought, because we soon learned that we were not prisoners of war but captives.

# 5

The Jap forces swarm all over Corregidor. We are herded together and made to sit on the ground with our hands over our heads. We were kept this way for about three days. No food or water. Rings, wristwatches, jewelry and any other items we have that strike the fancy of the Japs are stripped from us. Objections are met with a rifle butt to the face or body. It was not uncommon to see a Jap with seven or eight wristwatches on one arm. They snickered and laughed at us, treating us with the utmost oriental contempt, interspersed with blows from clubs or rifle butts...sometimes a bayonet.

We were eventually marched to an area on the beach called the 92nd garage area. The only shelter in the area was an old garage building that had been severely bombed and shelled out. POW numbers were painted on our shirts by the Japs. Many of us made shelters from the bombed debris in the area to provide us with some sort of relief from the torrid sun and the severe rainstorms experienced at that time of year.

For the first few days we were given no food or water.

I should mention at this time that we were approximately 12,000 men, of which about 9,000 were Americans and 3,000 Filipinos. There were also many hundreds of wounded and sick in the hospital in Malinta Tunnel along with 68 nurses. At a later date, the nurses were moved to Santo Tomas University and interned there for the duration of the war along with many civilian internees.

We were finally given rice twice a day, and water was found in the 92nd area. It was common to stand in line for hours and hours to fill your canteen with water. Some of the men had the foresight or luck to take some canned food with them upon capture, but in a few days' time it was all consumed. The only other food we had was what we could salvage while on work details for the Japs. If the Japs caught you "stealing" food, you would be severely beaten or, perhaps, killed.

We were put on work details cleaning up debris, burying the dead, etc. A sight to behold is a dead body that has been left out in the scorching tropical sun for a week or more. The body turns a purplish color and blows up to three or four times its natural size. Buttons burst, shoes split, and the body in time literally explodes from the accumulation of gases within it. The stench is awful; insects crawl through all the body openings; flies, in humming droves, swarm all over the body; rats and maggots leave their signatures. The sun blistered skin, and sometimes a leg or arm, would come off when you handled them. You think, could this putrescent mass have been a living person just weeks ago? The area looks like an abandoned junkyard with bodies scattered among the debris.

*Love one another as I love you?*
For Christ's sake, what the hell happened, God?

While there were many more Japanese than Americans killed on Corregidor, there were not as many of their bodies around, as it was Japanese custom to burn their dead immediately after battle and ship their ashes home. The few Japanese bodies we encountered evoked no emotion in me at that time. Their bodies looked the same as our dead and the dried up blood was the same color.

Don't be caught by American's honey words any longer.

You are already like a rat in a trap  If you continue resisting, you will

be drowned in the sea or die of starvation.

You shall be annihilated to the last man!

Come over to our side waving white cloth.

It is not the Japanese army alone which is waiting for you on this side,

but your parents, your wife, and your dear ones as well are longing

to see you behind our lines.

Leaflet dropped by Japanese during fighting on Bataan and Corregidor. March 1942

## Address of Instruction

It is entirely out of my expectations to see the betrayal, the most outrageous and unfortunate trouble that has been caused recently. Under the vast virtues of His Majesty the Emperor, all the personnel have treated you with sympathy, spirit of Bushido. But the very three escapees that have dared to go against my wishes may well be said to be absolutely inhuman.

When all of you try to complete your duty and responsibility peace and welfare will surely be in your hands. In fact, we have considered various means and have intended to consider in future for the benefit of your welfare. But you yourselves have quited your fortune and thrown yourselves into the state of Hell. We will no longer tolerate any trifling trouble and continue to make the strict surveillance over you up to the time when all of you start your life all over again and I am to punish not only one most strictly that should violate the above warning, but one's ten men group that are jointly responsible for one's misconduct.

Moreover I will never tolerate anyone who speaks tricks, lie or is insolent in his attitude.

June 29, 1943

Colonel M. Matsuda
Commandant of M. W. P. C.

Address by Col. Matsuda, Mukden Prison Camp, after escape by 3 prisoners, who were caught and executed.

# 6

I have been told that the easiest way to learn a foreign language is to get a "sleeping dictionary," i.e. some woman of foreign tongue, and live with her. There is an easier way, but not as much fun. Just become a Jap POW. They speak to you only in their language most of the time. They have effective teaching methods, although a bit unorthodox. If they shout *"Kiotsuki"* at you and you don't respond, a rifle butt to your face or body taught you that it meant "Attention." *"Kora"* meant "Hey you" and was the lowest form of recognition in their language. The first word I learned in Japanese was *"misu,"* meaning water. Then *"benjo,"* a Japanese vulgarism for toilet. I learned quite a few words in my early education as a Jap prisoner of war, and I have some high "marks" to prove it. If all men should be brothers, I have to pass on those guys.

It was not surprising that many of our men just laid down and gave up living. It was an easy escape from the horrors of further disease, starvation, Japanese cruelty, and things unknown to come. It is also not surprising that most, if not all, of the POWs who did survive still evidence hatred, hostility, and pent up anger towards many Japanese **of those times.**

I awoke one morning in the prison compound on Corregidor and discovered that all of my meager personal belongings were gone--stolen during the night by someone. I was shocked to think that some fellow POW was capable of such a contemptuous deed. Desperate men do desperate

19

things, I suppose. My valuables consisted of a spare set of clothes, a small bottle of salt, some sulfa pills (given to me by one of the nurses), reading glasses, a pipe, and a small tin of tobacco, canteen and mess kit, shaving material and toothbrush, and some treasured snapshots of my family. I hope the bastard got gingivitis using my toothbrush.

I guess, on or about the date we were captured human nature changed for some among us. It now was a world of survival of the fittest. Philosophically I mused that no matter how bad things were, they could get worse. I obtained a canteen and mess kit from one of the dead bodies. Thanks, old buddy, wherever you are.

Some two weeks later we were informed that we were moving. We were herded aboard some Japanese vessels in the bay and happily noted that we were sailing towards Manila and not Japan. Some hours later the vessels anchored in the bay and Jap landing craft unloaded us in the water some good distance from the shore. We had to jump into the water and wade ashore. The water reached almost up to my shoulders.

Sopping wet we reached shore, where we were lined up and marched through the streets of Manila, along Dewey Boulevard. The Japs, as usual, assisted us in the march in the real spirit of *Bushido* with blows from rifle butts or jabs from bayonets if you were slow, or perhaps it was a show for the Filipinos who lined the streets, sadly looking on. A cruel and ridiculous effort on the part of the Japs to assert their authority and superiority. A dismal failure.

The Filipinos lining the streets were grim faced and sad looking. Many had tears in their eyes as they beheld the "mighty conquerors" and their bedraggled captives. Some tossed us food, much to the chagrin of the guards, others whispered encouragements to us with tears in their eyes. Many of us were teary eyed too.

I don't remember how long we marched before we reached the gates of Bilibid prison. Bilibid was a prison

# Japan's Prisoner List of 1,036 Eases Fears for Missing Men

Mr. and Mrs. Conrad Bocksel, 1743 58th St. also felt a bit relieved when they were informed officially that their son, Chief Warrant Officer Arnold A. Bocksel, also is a prisoner.

"We were anxious, of course, but we all had a feeling he would come through all right," Mrs. Conrad Bocksel said. Young Bocksel had been stationed at Corregidor for only a few months before the war started.

## Escaped Nurse

When Helen Summers, Brooklyn nurse, who made her escape from the Philippines, reached home, she called on Mr. and Mrs. Bocksel to inform them that she had seen their son only a few days before she left. She reported that he was in good health and in excellent spirits. Some months later they received a letter from their son under date of May 3, three days before the fall of the fortress, bidding his family not to worry too much about him.

"I'm hitting on all six cylinders and changing the oil every 500 miles," he wrote them.

"There is plenty I can write, but cannot, so will ask you not to be unduly concerned over me."

Bocksel, who was born in Brooklyn 29 years ago, attended Manual Training High School and was graduated from the New York State Merchant Marine Academy. Soon after he became a marine engineer with the American Export Line and made numerous trips to outlying parts of the world. He went into the armed forces in February, 1941.

He has two brothers, Raymond, also a chief warrant officer with the army, and Lawrence, who, as a member of the Reserve Corps, is studying marine engineering at Pratt. There also is a sister, Mrs. Wheeler Crawford.

Chief Warrant Officer
Arnold A.

Newpaper clipping on author's capture.

Author's youngest brother, Buddy Bocksel, 20th Combat Engineers 1st Div. 8 Battle Stars, 2 Presidential Citations.

# 3 Stars Bloom In Tulip Bed of Brooklyn Yard

### Artist Honors Army Sons, One Held by Japanese, With 'V' Garden Design

A three-star tulip bed, planted last autumn by Conrad Bocksel to honor his three Army sons, one of them a Japanese prisoner, is bursting into bloom this week under a blossoming magnolia tree in the Bocksel front yard at 1743 Fifty-eighth Street, Brooklyn.

Mr. Bocksel, a professional artist and decorator whose hobby is gardening, laid out a large "V" with yellow tulips. Inside the "V" and on each side of it are stars of pink tulips.

The bulbs, which were imported from England, may have to serve for the duration, Mr. Bocksel believes, for Holland bulbs have been impossible to get since the war's beginning and English bulbs are rare.

The bed was planted four months after the last word had been received from the Bocksels' oldest son, Chief Warrant Officer Arnold A. Bocksel, twenty-nine, who served on the Army mine planter on Corregidor when it fell.

"Those pink tulips are evidence of our faith that he was not dead," Mrs. Bocksel said yesterday "Though things looked very dark we never lost our trust in God and our belief that he would return to us. On Christmas Eve I prayed especially hard at church, and on New Year's Eve we received a letter from the government telling us Arnold was a Japanese prisoner. I believe my prayers brought that letter."

A second son, Chief Warrant Officer Raymond Bocksel, twenty-six, stationed in Boston, is also an Army mine planter who, his mother said, "plants victory gardens in the sea." Both Arnold and Raymond were merchant seamen for six years before they enlisted in the Army two years ago. They are graduates of the New York State Merchant Marine Academy at Fort Schuyler, the Bronx.

The youngest son, Lawrence, nineteen, is a member of the Army Reserve Corps and is studying marine engineering at Pratt Institute, 215 Ryerson Street, Brooklyn.

Mrs. Bocksel doesn't permit herself time to worry about her sons. "I think it is better to stand behind them on the home front," she said. "Work in the Red Cross and at church keeps my mind off worries."

built by the Spaniards in the early 1800s. The only good thing I can say about it was that water was available there and the concrete floors we slept on were relatively clean. We were fed rice twice a day with some form of watery soup. It tasted good to hungry men...anything that was edible tasted good for the next three and one half years.

It was here that I made some real good friends, all from the 17th Pursuit Squadron, as well as a priest, Father Dick Carberry. The pilots, Jim Philipps, Earl Hulsey, Dick Carberry, Silas Wolf, were all great guys to be with. Always with a smile, great attitudes and genuine warmth. Jim was shot down over Manila Bay and had the stigmata of a P-38 crash emblazoned on his forehead over his right eye; a deep "U" shaped scar caused by his head crashing into the gun mount. Many pilots carried this same signature of a P-38 crash. It was not ugly, it was a badge of valor. With the exception of one, they were all killed on Japanese "Hell Ships" transporting them to Japan in late 1944. Unmarked ships that were, unfortunately, bombed by our Air Force.

And, dear Father Carberry, wherever you may be now, thanks again for the gift of those treasured sulfa pills when I probably would have died from dysentery. I shouldn't say "wherever you may be," because I know where you are--with the Being you personified and whose precepts you followed. *"Love one another, as I love you,"* and *"Greater love than this has no man...."* I can't bear to think that you may have died from dysentery because you had no sulfa pills yourself.

7

Some weeks later we were marched from Bilibid Prison to a railroad station for loading on the box cars, which I had mentioned at the start of this narrative. As I recall, we marched about 10 miles to the station. We were taken to another prison camp in Northern Luzon, Cabanatuan POW Camp.

We were loaded aboard the box cars, about 100 men to a car. It was rough sitting on the floor, bodies pressed close together, unable to move at all, temperature hovering well above the 100 degree mark, and no room to read a newspaper or do a crossword puzzle!

The toilet facilities were nonexistent. Put 100 men in a box car with most of them suffering from dysentery and you have a problem. We just used the floor of the train. At least you didn't have to wait on line. To be fair, even if toilet facilities had been available, most of us would not have been able to make it anyway. And, frankly, none of us cared at this point. We were bewildered and confused in the uncertainty of not knowing what was going to happen to us. We were existing in a dimension that was alien to any other previous experience of ours. A lot of water poured under the proverbial bridge while we pondered our predicament. I thought about the song that country songwriter Hank Williams wrote, called *"I don't care if tomorrow never comes...."* I agreed with him. The inexorability of our situation was strongly impacting upon us. I realized, now I had truly lost my innocence, and not at age

18, as I had thought. It was a rude awakening. When you thought about tomorrow, you almost hated to see the sun rise.

The blood stained fecal excreta or shit was interesting and sometimes fascinating to observe as it intermingled with urine and formed myriad patterns on the floor of the train. One man's foot retards the flow, another's hand deflects it, someone's cheek stops it, and someone's chin divides it. I wondered if a Gypsy could tell fortunes from the patterns on the floor.

You sit in it; get it on your hands, your face, your clothes; some poor devil has his face in it and just stays that way. "Christ," is this a dream, a nightmare?--No, buddy, you are, to put it simply, in the middle of history in a sea of shit.

Thank God, they didn't give us any food this trip. We would have eaten it.

The only air we got was through a two-inch crack in the doors. If someone was in severe distress, we would shift around and let him breathe through the door opening...that is, if he didn't die before we could shift around.

You don't know how long you have been in the box car, but it feels like a lifetime. Blissfully, you return to some semblance of reality when you hear the train grinding to a stop. Japs are screaming and the doors are opened. You feel air--beautiful, beautiful air, and you just lift your head and breathe and breathe. You hold it in your lungs and slowly exhale, and slowly breathe and exhale...you are having an orgy with air...and you know it is better than sex.

The Cabanatual Express has completed her run. We are unloaded and told we will sleep in holding pens. I presumed that these were originally pens for livestock. I am right. We are also told that tomorrow morning we will be marched to the new prison camp.

We get a ball of rice and are shoved into the pens, surrounded by barbed wire and mean grunting guards. We find that the pens have been used for previously transported prisoners. The ground is soggy and the odor pungent, and we find ourselves in a quagmire of feces, blood, and urine, with maggots added for flavor. And there is no other place to sleep but in it. It's a miasma of unbelievable reality. I knew then what the person meant who said, *"Stop the world, I want to get off!"*

Somehow we survived again, but what little morale was left eroded swiftly.

Almost every Japanese controlled prisoner of war march was a so-called "Death March." All of us were participants in many of these marches throughout the years of imprisonment.

The first and best known was the "Bataan Death March," probably the worst of all. Ruthless, cruel, inhuman guards forced prisoners to march from Bataan to Camp O'Donnell, a distance of approximately 140 miles for some. No food, water, or protection from the scorching sun was provided. Men were continually beaten along the line of march and many were executed. The pain filled journey took approximately 1,000 American and thousands of Filipino lives.

A sad saga of Japanese hatred toward exhausted, sick and honorable men.

Over 1,300 men packed into 10 freight cars. Sketch by Col. E. Jacobs

# 8

In the morning we started on our march to the new prison camp. We were given a rice ball for breakfast. They say, it is better to march on an empty stomach and I wished that the person who had said that was marching with us.

My God, but it was hot marching, and the air was full of a powder-like dust from the dry, parched roads. The dust permeates the air, giving it a gritty taste. You plod along somehow...staring at the dirt road almost hypnotized...no one is talking much...one foot ahead of the other...right foot...left foot...move...move...move...breathe slowly...breathe...only it starts to hurt...so much grit and dust in the air...the damn scorching sun...better sip some water, no, not much...save it...just a little sip more...a prod with a rifle butt reminds you that you are not moving fast enough...Goddamn it, that hurts. Those who fall out, I don't know what happens to them...and if I fall out I don't give a damn what happens to me.

They let us rest for a while that afternoon. No food. Water getting low. The combination of dust and perspiration makes us a motley looking crew, even to each other. Sweat covered faces streaked where perspiration has cleared paths through the covering dust; eyes wild, reflecting misery; exhausted, aching bodies. Some men run to the side of the road where carabao are wallowing in muddy water (carabao are beasts of burden, of the water buffalo family). Those men fill their canteens from the muddy waters. Even the carabao look astonished. Thirst crazed men don't care. It was suicidal...and I think many of them knew it. Jap guards laugh at them. These are really nice guys. Others might have shot them as they did on the Bataan Death March, earlier in our capture. Lucky again.

We were still marching late in the day. We passed some Filipinos who threw pieces of sugar cane at us. Some of the lucky ones grasped the cane as it was thrown. It was a great source of energy--and we later learned that it has a laxative effect, which we needed like a hole in the head.

I think we had marched about 12 miles. Jim alongside me. We didn't talk much, trying to conserve energy. Someone said to suck on a pebble to alleviate your thirst; didn't do a thing for me. Every once in a while a man fell out and surprisingly the Japs don't bayonet or shoot him as they did on previous marches, and as I said, they took no punitive action against the men who ran to the carabao wallows. I am beginning to believe that we are the luckiest guys in the world.

You look around at Jim Phillips who is plodding along beside you and you see that he has his arm around the waist of the man next to him and they are both stumbling along. The man he is aiding is an older man. He has tears in his eyes as he tells Jim to let him go...it's every man for himself now, he says. You look over at Jim and say to yourself, this crazy bastard is going to get us all killed, as you shift to the other side of the man and grab him around the waist, too. That idiot Jim looks at you and grins. How did I ever get mixed up with such a weak and stupid character? You look at him, shake your head, and break out in a grin, too. You remember something about united we stand or fall, and start to laugh.

We finally reach the camp at dusk. All you want to do is get some water and lie down. Yep, you guessed it...no water in the camp. The Japs say they were told water was in the camp. To be honest, they looked rather thirsty too. They say, tomorrow we march to another camp nearby where there is water. For now, no water--nothing.

You fall into a heap on the ground and enter into some sort of state of animated suspension where you dream of water; ice; ice cold lemonade; icebergs; coke; Niagara Falls; and the Atlantic Ocean.

Sometime later you come to with a start. Was that a drop of water you felt on your face or just a bird flying overhead? You look up, and miracle of miracles, you behold gorgeously beautiful, gloriously ominous black clouds approaching. You hold your breath and just say, *"Please God, please."*

With streaks of lightning illuminating the way, thunderous roaring announcing their coming, the black clouds approach overhead. At some ethereal command they come to the magnificent position of "halt" directly overhead. Water from the heavens burst forth. You take off your clothes so you can feel the water on your skin; you run under the eaves of a Nipa hut with a bamboo roof and drink from the many rivulets of water flowing down. You are having another orgy, this time with water. Jim says, I hope I don't wake up and find this a dream. I say, if it is a dream, I hope I never wake up.

I can't say "lucky" this time...I think a lot of prayers were answered. After all, we were still alive, the evening was cool, the ground was clean, and the Japs gave us a rice ball for supper. How many people have it so good?

In the morning we were marched to another camp, fortunately only several hours distance. The new camp has lots of water. We were housed in old bamboo huts with thatched roofs. The bunks were shelves of split bamboo. No water or toilet facilities in the huts and about 100 men to each hut. There were upper and lower shelves of bamboo slats for sleeping. They were always damp, with shrubs of mildew sprouting everywhere.

Rice was the main staple of our diet. A watery rice in the morning, called lugao; then plain rice for lunch, and

27

a watery soup with rice in the evening. The soup contained some vegetable leaves and once in a while we got soup with carabao meat in it. If you ever found a piece of meat in your soup as big as your small fingernail, you had hit the jackpot.

Deprivation of food was a weapon deliberately used by the Japs to keep prisoners in a weakened condition and to break down morale. Weakened and sick men cause less problems; lose their aggressiveness and actually become docile. Weakened men are also less likely to attempt escape. The Nazis used these same tactics in their concentration camps, that is, until they invented a quicker and more efficient means of dealing with the inmates...gas chambers.

The following is an excerpt from the *Japan Times* newspaper published in 1942, sometimes after the surrender of Bataan:

> *...they, the Allies surrender after sacrificing all the lives they can, except their own, for a cause which they know well is futile. They have shown themselves to be utterly selfish throughout all the campaigns, the Commandments of God, and their defeat is their punishment. To show them mercy is to prolong the war. Their motto has been "Absolute Unscrupulousness." They have not cared what means they employed in their operations. An eye for an eye, a tooth for a tooth. The Japanese are crusaders in a Holy War. Hesitation is uncalled for and the wrong-doers must be wiped out.*

You were right about one thing, we were trying to kill you bastards, the same way you were trying to kill us, only we didn't use *Bushido* methods, thank God.

Perhaps Kipling was right when he said, *"East is East*

*and West is West, and never the twain shall meet."*

You Japanese were culturally different from us; your sense of ethics was different from ours; you have shown that you did not have the same compassion and understanding towards your fellow man that we had (unless he is Japanese); you felt that warriors must commit suicide rather than be captured by the enemy, solely because you considered it a sure way of entering your heaven; and your dishonesty and deception were first evidenced at the "diplomatic" talks between the Japanese Ambassador to the U.S. and our U.S. Secretary of State in December of 1941. While the talks were going on, your forces were enroute to Pearl Harbor and the Philippines!

And you had the audacity to call yourselves "Crusaders in a Holy War"??? Check out your holy crusade with the men you murdered at Pearl Harbor, or with the thousands of your WWII captives: American, Filipinos, British, Dutch, Australians, and those you warred against in China and Korea in your attempted conquest of Southeast Asia. I'll tell you "holy crusaders" one thing, no one will ever genuflect before you.

General McArthur wrote, *"your actions were a stain upon civilization and constitute a memory of shame and dishonor that can never be forgotten."*

The Potsdam Declaration specified, *"Stern justice shall be meted out to all war criminals, including those who have visited cruelties upon prisoners."*

Your actions forever blot out the honor of Japanese troops. The courageous men you captured deserved, at least, the honors of warriors in their hour of defeat. Holy Crusade?; Holy Cow!, as Phil Rizzuto would say.

In fairness, I must say that I encountered some Japanese of noble character during my incarceration. These I discuss later on in this narrative. My remarks at this time are primarily intended for those Japanese, at that time, in those places. I have no vituperation toward the Japanese of these times. The children cannot be accountable for the sins of their fathers.

I can even forgive them for what they did to me, though I can never forget. It is like a serious wound that has healed and left an ugly scar. I forgive them, because my religious beliefs tell me so. I cannot forgive them, however, for those who perished in their prison camps as a result of their cruel treatment. They will have to ask them for forgiveness one day, when and if they meet again.

(National Archives)
A group of American POW's at the start of the Bataan Death March. April 1942.

*9*

---

Escape was always on our minds. It was a difficult situation, primarily due to the weakened condition we all experienced from sickness and starvation. Three men attempted escape one evening in Cabanatuan prison camp. They were quickly apprehended by the Japs who, after beating them severely, tied them to wooden stakes outside the prison compound, where they were in view of the other prisoners inside the compound. They were kept there for three days with no food or water, continually exposed to the scorching sun and regularly beaten by the Japanese. It was a terrible sight to behold and all that the Japs accomplished was to increase our hatred of them. However, the Japs could be merciful at times, and they were this time, they executed them. As I recall, one was beheaded and the other two shot. The whole incident was probably intended as a graphic example of what would happen to any prisoner planning to escape. To further insure against any escapes, they divided us into groups of ten men. If any man in the group of ten escaped, the other nine would be executed. Clever bastards. I wondered if they said "so solly" when they cut your head off. Out of one 10 man group it was reported that the remaining 9 were executed when the one escaped.

The Japanese art of decapitation was practiced by placing the victim in a kneeling position, with the head bowed down. The big brave Samurai Executioner raises his sword high in the air, holding it in both hands, and with a

31

blood curdling scream swishes down and through the neck. Custom decrees that a good executioner will always complete the beheading with only one stroke or he might "lose face" (no pun intended). I could tell you more about Japanese culture, but right now I am nauseous.

Another thing about decapitation is that it is fast. If you are ever going to be decapitated, always try to be the first. You avoid the interminable waiting and the blade is sharper.

Flies were another enemy we encountered in prison camp. Droves and droves of them flitting from the open latrines to our mess kits, our hands, faces, and every part of our exposed body. We were constantly shooing them away. It was pitiful to see a dying man, face and hands encrusted with those goddamn flies, and he oblivious to their presence. They undoubtedly were one of the primary causes for the overwhelming incidence of dysentery spreading among us. Most of us learned to place a piece of cloth over our mess kit and slide the spoon under it while eating. It was the only effective way to keep the thousands of flies that milled about off the food. They were one of our worst enemies in prison camp.

Toilet tissue was a nonexistent item. Most of us used a cloth for these purposes, washing it out after each use; and it was a common sight to see these stained banners drying outside of each barrack. When you had a severe case of dysentery, you didn't use anything at all. It was too painful to touch those personal parts.

Chair and benches did not exist in camp. From the Filipinos we learned to sit in a squatting position with our arms around our knees and rear ends just off the ground. We could assume this position for hours in our "bull" sessions though it was difficult to stand for a while after arising from the squatting position.

A tin can was a valuable possession. You could store reserve water in it; but primarily it was used in the art of

*"Quanning,"* and carried by many with a rope tied around their waist. The *"quan"* can was used to cook any items of food that you might acquire during the day. The word *"Quan"* is a Filipino word, roughly translated into "stew." Snails, lizards, and snakes, mixed with the leaves of camotes (sweet potatoes), wild onions, and any other items you might gather that were considered edible. Men volunteered for working details outside the camp just for the possibility of acquiring food for their quan. They often pooled these food items and cooked their quan in the tin cans as in the days of old, when hobos cooked their mulligan after a day of scrounging. Snake was a delicacy in the quan can.

September, 1942. The naked dead, carried on window blinds to burial. Sketch by Col. E. Jacobs.

Execution of three American Prisoners of War for attempted escape. Cabanatuan POW Camp, Philippines.
(National Archives)

American Prisoners of War at time of liberation.
(National Archives)

# 10

Dysentery was by far the greatest killer in our midst, especially in the first years of our capture. We were burying as many as 40-50 men a day during the first six months of captivity. In Cabanatuan Prison Camp in the Philippines, 2,300 prisoners died by the end of 1942, after eight months of captivity. In O'Donnel Prison Camp, following the Bataan Death March, 1,600 Americans and untold thousands of Filipinos died within a six week period. It was difficult to find men physically capable of carrying the dead to the makeshift graves.

In Cabanatuan, the grave detail gathered the bodies of those who had died the day before and on makeshift litters, made of tree limbs and blankets, carried them to the burial grounds--a large ditch dug in the ground. The litter bearers were nothing but walking cadavers themselves. The bodies were thrown into the large pits, one on top of the other. In the rainy season, legs, arms, and other parts would protrude from the ground and had to be recovered with dirt.

I always said a prayer as the dead passed by on their way to the burial ground, and many of us shed a tear...but, I really don't know if it was for them or ourselves, wondering when our turn would come. The spectre of death was omnipresent.

In an attempt to be objective in this narrative (which is extremely difficult), I would point out--though not in defense of the Japanese--that our forces at the time of capture were in weakened physical condition. Rations had been cut in half and then to a quarter on Bataan and Corregidor. Malaria and other sicknesses were rampant among our forces and taking their toll among the Defenders. In addition, many of the men were wounded when captured.

General Wainwright radioed President Roosevelt in March 1942 that if help was not forthcoming, Bataan would be starved into submission.

The point is made, objectively, that we were in extremely poor physical condition at the time of surrender. For the Japanese to subject these men to cruel and inhuman treatment was inexcusable.

As I have stated, they were angry and hateful of us because the stubborn defense by the Defenders caused the Japs to abandon their frontal attacks, which had become very costly to them. It had been reported that the Jap Commander, General Homma, even considered abandonment of the original plan to capture the Philippines in favor of bypassing it, in order to keep up with the Jap timetable for the conquest of Southeast Asia.

The American forces in the Philippines were primarily starved into capitulation.

* * * * * * * * *

Charcoal is great for barbecues, it is also great for dysentery. With dysentery at its peak, you are having as many as 20 to 30 or more bowel movements daily, primarily of blood and mucous. At this point, you don't have much longer to live, and what's worse, you don't give a damn. You lie around with your lower half naked, or with a gunny sack tied around your middle, if you are shy. I've seen men go from 120 lbs. in weight to 70-80 lbs. in a matter of a week or two. The only treatment available is to go to one of the burned out fires and grab a piece of charcoal and chew on it slowly; or, if you can obtain some leaves from a guava tree, to make a brew out of it. I believe it contained tannic acid which was helpful. But sorry, Buddy, you are going to die anyway. The charcoal will help relieve some of the cramps, but nothing else. A few of the luckier ones among us survived; I suppose they were stronger too; I was among them.

As one who has had dysentery, I can tell you it is difficult to live among people afflicted with it...that is in a prison camp. We slept on two tiered shelves and if you didn't get an upper, you were in trouble. Many a morning those on the lower bunks would awaken and find themselves covered in bloody feces from some poor devil above them. A young Lieutenant, who slept next to me in Cabanatuan--I forgot his name--came down with severe dysentery. A few days later he was wearing a gunny sack, two days later I leaned over to shake him awake in the morning, his eyes were wide open, and he was staring fixedly above him. He was dead. I cried so much that morning, and I am so ashamed that I can't even remember his name, but I will never forget his face.

Another manifestation of our deficient rice diet was what we called "Rice Belly." A distension of the stomach or pot belly. It was ludicrous to see a 100 lb. man with a large protruding stomach. From a distance, you would have thought that there were a lot of pregnant women in our midst.

Vitamin C was severely lacking in our diet. Many of us would chew the Filipino grass (cogon) in the hopes of extracting some vitamin C from it. We would spit it out after chewing it for a while. Sometimes, on a work detail, if you were lucky and cunning you might find a piece of fruit fallen from a bush or tree. Sometimes a coconut, bananas, or mangos. Biting into a fresh mango is a form of ecstasy you never forget.

Have a toothache? No problem. See the American doctor in prison camp, that is, if you are lucky enough to have a doctor in your camp. The only dental procedure he can follow is to extract the tooth, if he can, using an ordinary pair of pliers, just like the kind you have in your tool box--you will get a nightmare of instant relief. In a Jap prison camp, anesthesia is just a word in the dictionary. Hospital is just a delay on the journey to your grave.

Beriberi is a rough disease to have in a prison camp. It apparently develops from lack of proteins and thiamine. With wet beriberi, the legs swell to elephantine proportions and the body becomes bloated to such an extent that features are often unrecognizable. The pain is so severe that brave men cry. Vitamin B prevents it, and the way to avoid it is to eat a diet containing meat, fish, beans, etc. Vitamin B is also available in the husks discarded in polishing rice. These husks are fed to livestock. It took us several years of importuning the Japs and convincing them to supply us with this fodder--that is, in the prison camp I was in. Most other prison camps did not receive these huskings. We used to sprinkle it on our morning cornmeal.

In the POW camp in Manchuria, where I was later imprisoned, cornmeal was the staple of our diet, sometimes, at the beginning, three times a day. It also is the staple of the Manchurians who have some kind of morning greeting which roughly translates to, *"Have you had your cornmeal today?"*

Our doctors sometimes performed a sympathectomy in the most severe cases, a surgical procedure in which the nerves leading to the legs are severed and the patient is free of pain and any further feelings in his legs. The legs are still swollen and you had better be damn careful that they don't freeze on you in the winter, which is most of the time in Northern Manchuria, some few hundred miles from Siberia. We often experienced temperatures of up to -45 degrees F. It was so cold at times that if you were on an outside work detail, the secretion from your nose would form into icicles, giving you the appearance of a walrus.

Did any of you men ever experience an itching,

burning, tender to the touch sensation in your testicles? And I don't mean from you know what! Well, if you are in a Jap prison camp and experience these symptoms, you have some vitamin deficiency disease. Other symptoms are a raw and sore tongue, and raw and sore testicles. It is quite painful. The skin of the scrotum actually sloughs away. Some of the men devised small slings (in some cases, large!) to keep these valued appendages from rubbing against the body and aggravating the condition. The Japs decided to treat us for this. They lined us up and painted our testicles with iodine! After the first scream I said, *"there go the family jewels."* Someone else remarked, *"I thought, only monkeys had red balls."* Their treatment didn't cure a thing.

We had many real heroes in prison camp. They didn't get any special medals for their heroic acts. These were the men who carried the sick with dysentery to the latrines, washed and cleansed them too; brushed away the ever present flies and held their hands when they were dying. They also answered when they called for God or Mama, and closed their eyes when they died--and cried a little, too. I once heard a man cry in his delirium, "Mama, Mama, please take care of me, come and get me, Mama... Mama....Mama."

These heroes were the same men who gave you a few grains of quinine, that they were saving for themselves, when your malaria got bad. These were the men who shared sips of their water with you, when you had none. These were the men who helped you make it when you were on one of the infamous marches. These were the men who gave away other medicines they had so you might live. And many of them died for want of the same medicines they gave away. These were the men who gave comfort and love when it was desperately needed. These were the real heroes...those who lived the Beatitudes. They have a very special place in "Soldiers' Heaven."

Work details in the Philippines, while I was there, consisted of road clearing, wood details to obtain firewood, cleaning the brush, etc. Beatings from the Japs were common for any infraction, real or imagined. The Japs carried small clubs which they used indiscriminately for any cause that suited their fancy. We had to stand rigidly at attention if they addressed us and bow to them in their presence. Any time one of them came into our quarters someone had to shout *"Kiotsuki"* (attention) and we would stand at attention and bow deeply from the waist. In the mornings, we had to line up for roll call *(Tenko)* and count off in Japanese. An error in shouting your number general-- ly meant a blow or two to the face. Obviously, we learned to count in Japanese quickly and fluently. We also had to learn the servile form of Japanese. For example, "thank you" in Japanese is *"Arigato"* and "good morning" is *"Ohaiyo,"* pronounced Ohio, that is, for persons of the same social stratum. The servile or very polite form is to add *"gozaimasu"* as in *"Ohaiyo-gozaimasu,"* and *"Arigato-gozaimasu."* Same as saying "Thank you, honorable one," or "Good morning, honorable one."

Now that you know a little Japanese, I hope you never have to use the servile form.

While I have previously discussed the brutality of the Japs towards their prisoners, it was far more brutal during our early capture and on the many marches we endured. Their cruelness and brutality were manifested in the sadism with which they treated us. What upset me most was their utter disregard of us as human beings and members of the human race. They exhibited sheer pleasure in venting their anger on helpless prisoners of war. As I have said, they hated us and in their moment of temporary control over their enemies, manifested their "superiority" in the only manner they knew--or wanted to know.

Not every prisoner was beaten on the hour every day. One might go for days, weeks, or even months without being beaten, provided you didn't run afoul of them; but you can bet that some Jap prisoners in some Jap prison camp were beaten or abused every single day of captivity.

The "Zero" Ward of Cabanatuan prison hospital received terminally ill or mortally wounded United States soldiers. Sketch by Col. E. Jacobs, Former POW.

*12*

It is October, 1942 in Cabanatuan POW Camp, and rumors are rampant. We call them "Latrine O'Grams":

*Ford Motor Co. is going to give each prisoner of war, when repatriated; new car.*

*A special task force is on its way to the Philippines solely to rescue us.*

*The Marines have already landed in the Philippines on a POW rescue mission.*

*The Red Cross is arranging for an exchange of POWs.*

*The Japs are going to give us a hamburger a day.*

And so on and so on. Sadly, many of the men believed these rumors.

One day my name was called. I was informed that I was in a group of 2,000 men being transferred to prison camps in Manchuria. I was among the 16 officers assigned to this group. I didn't want to go, but I had no choice in the matter. The next day, after sad and tearful eyes of farewell to my close buddies, we were marched to the docks in Manila. We were loaded on board a Jap freighter, the

41

WA83 55 US GOVT=WUX WASHINGTON DC 26 227A

MRS ANGELA BUCKSEL=

1743 56TH ST BROOKLYN NY=

THE NAME OF WARRANT OFFICER ARNOLD J BUCKSEL HAS BEEN
MENTIONED IN AN ENEMY BROADCAST AS A PRISONER IN JAPANESE
HANDS THE PURPOSE OF SUCH BROADCASTS IS TO GAIN LISTENERS
FOR THE ENEMY PROPAGANDA WHICH THEY CONTAIN BUT THE ARMY
IS CHECKING THE ACCURACY OF THIS INFORMATION AND WILL
ADVISE YOU AS SOON AS POSSIBLE=

FOREIGN BROADCAST INTELLIGENCE SERVICE OF FEDERAL

COMMUNICATIONS COMMISSION.

1943 DEC 26 AM 3 10

First message received regarding status of author; some 20 months after capture.

vfj

**WAR DEPARTMENT**

THE ADJUTANT GENERAL'S OFFICE

WASHINGTON

IN REPLY
REFER TO  AG 201  Bocksel, Arnold Armand
(12-2--42)  PC-G 360053

January 6, 1943.

*Received 20 months after Capture*

Mrs. Conrad Bocksel,
1743 58th Street,
Brooklyn, New York.

Dear Mrs. Bocksel:

Report has been received that your___son,
Warrant Officer Arnold Armand Bocksel, W-901,770,
is now a prisoner of war of the Japanese Government in the Philippine
Islands. This will confirm my telegram of December 29, 1942.

The Provost Marshal General, Prisoner of War Information
Bureau, Washington, D.C., will furnish you the address to which mail may
be sent. Any future correspondence in connection with his status as a
prisoner of war should be addressed to that office.

Very truly yours,

J. A. ULIO
Major General,
The Adjutant General

*MIA- 1 YR 8mos*

1 Inclosure
Memorandum re financial benefits.

"Tatori Maru." We called it the *"Diarrhea Maru."* The vessel had no Red Cross markings on it, nor any other markings to designate it as carrying POWs. A direct violation of the Geneva Convention rules for transporting prisoners of war.

We were berthed in the lower holds of the vessel, on the steel deck plates. The scorching sun, fetid air, pungent odors, and the jammed overcrowding were a far cry from even a cattle boat. I learned what Dante's Inferno must have felt like.

Our American commanding officer was a Major Stanley Hankins. He was from a small town in Kentucky and a Corporal or Sergeant at the commencement of hostilities, as well as a reserve officer. He quickly rose to the rank of Major on Bataan. He was one of the most clever and brilliant officers I encountered in the service. Apparently he had a problem with alcohol; however, in the absence of alcohol in our prison environment, his true brilliance surfaced. We were very fortunate to have him as our leader.

As soon as we boarded the vessel, he notified me that I was the Mess Officer. I was shocked because I had had no experience in the culinary arts. I was an engineer. However, I reasoned you can only cook rice one way, with water. I also knew how to cook eggs but there was little chance of ever seeing those again. I remembered a recipe I once read on how to make a delicious Mexican omelette:

*"First, steal six eggs...."*

I reported to some Jap on deck who showed me the cooking area assigned to us. There were two large cauldrons and, surprise of surprises, lots of rice, carrots, potatoes, and a small amount of meat. It was unbelievable.

I gathered a group of men who were cooks in the service and decided the only way to equitably distribute the

42

food was in the form of soup. The men had a real treat that evening, even though the portions were small. I would say, the best meal since our capture. Apparently, the Japanese merchant seaman had not been advised of the meager amount of food to be meted out to us. We received these same type rations for a few days and then we were suddenly back to our old diet.

We steamed towards Formosa, where we were to drop off our sick and dead; by sick I mean those who were apparently dying. As I recall, only 11 or 12 men died on the ship; however, many or most of those we left in Formosa succumbed.

As I have previously mentioned, I can understand some of the anger and brutality vented upon us when we were first captured. We had killed a lot of them and their timetable for further conquests had been seriously delayed by at least six months by the stubborn defense of the forces on Bataan and Corregidor. The Jap commanders and their front line troops were angry at us and furthermore, had lost face with the military command in Tokyo. (To a Jap, losing face is worse than coming home unexpectedly and finding his wife in bed with another man.)

I admit that what I learned about Japanese culture, philosophy, Shintoism, and customs was learned in prejudiced circumstances. However, close association is often a knowing teacher. Like all of us, Japs were the products of their environment, culture and religion which embodied fanaticism and mythological stories or legends. For instance, their code of chivalry, which demanded honor above life. This, no doubt, accounted for their fearless fighting, their suicidal missions, and their dedication to their war effort.

While I feel that all religions promulgate goodness, charity, kindness and love of fellow man, I still am confused about some of their values. I admit that in warfare, in the heat of battle, these concepts are difficult to practice on an enemy by anyone. However, once an enemy becomes your

43

prisoner, there is no valid reasoning to justify cruelty and brutality. Hate is not a good excuse.

Any honorable soldier who has been in combat knows that after the battle is over, when the noise, dust, screams, and smoke have ceased, he should lean over and give his conquered foe his hand. Common ordinary decency dictates this among the world family of mankind. None of these concepts were practiced by the horde of Japanese conquerors of the Philippines. I respect an enemy force that exercises the concepts of loyalty, faith, honor, self-sacrifice, courage, duty, and patriotism, but they must also have decency and compassion.

The Geneva Convention specifically dictates the treatment for Prisoners of War. Why the Japanese refused to follow the dictates of this instrument we shall probably never know. They say, the true spirit of the Nipponese soldier is embodied in the practice of loyalty, filial spirit, and the dedication to fight and lay down his life to exalt the illustrious virtues of His Imperial Majesty, the Emperor, the descendent of the Sun Goddess. This philosophy may make a good soldier, but it sure makes a lousy captor.

The policy of POW treatment emanated from the Imperial Japanese headquarters in Tokyo. Prisoners were to be subjugated, and under no circumstances allowed to be retaken by their forces. It is to this group that I primarily direct my vituperation. Undoubtedly, not all of the abuses against prisoners were dictated by Tokyo, but by their neglect and apparent unconcern they are guilty...guilty.

The Japanese basically had contempt and scorn for anyone becoming a prisoner of war. It is contrary to the *Bushido* code to be captured by an enemy. However, they forgot that anyone who was captured was a combatant: a soldier in the thick of battle, often wounded; a sailor plucked from the high seas off a sinking vessel; or an airman shot down over enemy territory. These men were not war criminals, they were men of honor, taken in the heat of battle while fighting for their country. We did not expect to be honored, but we did expect our Japanese victors to recognize and respect our dignity and our rights as human beings. At that time, you Japanese had a great opportunity to show the world your compassion, honor and humanity when you had absolute power over your captives...but, you blew it.

To beat and kill helpless men on your "death marches"; to deprive men of the basic necessities of life-- food, water, basic medicines; to allow men to die of malaria, dengue fever, dysentery, scurvy, pellagra and diphtheria; to provide no pain killing drugs--just because we were your captives who opposed you in a war that you started, is a rotten way to practice *Bushido*.

You had better change your image before you start another war. As someone said, "no one may come."

In the hold, tropical underwear in the winter. Sketch by Col. E. Jacobs.

# 13

After we left Formosa, we nervously steamed onward towards Kobe, Japan. Approximately 500 of our men were disembarked. The remainder steamed on to Pusan, Korea.

Sometime earlier, Major Hankins convinced the Japs to let the men sleep on the open decks, which was like heaven compared to the conditions in the holds.

It was early November 1942, and the cold weather we were experiencing was taking its toll among us. The only clothing we had was the tropical clothing we had worn in the Philippines. Believe it or not, many of the men returned to the holds for the warmth generated by their body heat.

In the cold weather it was also an ordeal to use the makeshift latrines temporarily constructed on the main deck. Long, open wooden troughs, the length of the aft-deck, and continually flushed by running sea water. You practically got a salt water enema every time you used it, which was often, with the dysentery we were experiencing. I reasoned, however, if a salt water gargle was good for your throat, it must do wonders for your ass.

Another luxury item furnished us on this voyage was toilet tissue. Try going without it for a long, long time, and you will know what I mean. I'm sure, lack of sanitation in this regard was a causal factor in our high death rate. If I had to do it over again, I would recommend using your left hand for wiping and your right hand for eating. There actually is a culture that practices this: the Afghanistans. They use their left hand for personal body functions and their right hand for eating; primarily because it is customary for them to eat out of one communal pot, dipping into it for food with their right hand.

I wonder what Afghan men do who have had their right hand cut off for crimes like stealing? Interesting thought.

In India, they also have this same custom of eating with their fingers out of a common pot. One Indian, when asked why they did not use forks or spoons, replied that it would be like making love through an interpreter.

These American POW's are about to embark on a
Japanese hell-ship going to Japan from the Philippines.

# 14

We finally arrived in Pusan, Korea, about one month after we had left the Philippines. We were hungry again and shivering to death because of the cold weather. We were turned over to another unit of the Japanese Army, the Kwantung Army in Manchuria. They were the Japanese Army that had conquered Manchuria some years previously and had been fighting in Northern China for years.

Much to our consternation, we were ordered to strip off our clothes and--I thought--here it is, we are starting all over again. Instead of the hot sun, we are going to get the freezing cold treatment. I was so cold that I even yearned for the warmth of the box cars or the warmth of the crowded ship's holds.

We were marched a short distance to a warehouse where to our astonishment and utter disbelief we were issued old Chinese army clothing. Padded trousers, padded shirts or jackets, woolen underwear, old boots, and over-coats. We just couldn't believe it, we were so bewildered. There was a jubilant air among us, sick as we were, and the rumors started again..."the war is over and they are dressing us up for repatriation."

We were then marched to a train with wooden seats for us, and each man was given a small box lunch of fish, carrots pickled in some sort of brine, and rice with soy sauce. Christ, maybe these rumors about the war being over are true!

We were on the train for two days, as I now recall,

enroute to Manchuria. Again, unbelievably, box lunches for food, and we were even given hot tea. I thought and decided I had died and gone to heaven. I wished I could have stayed on that train for the rest of the war.

We finally arrived in Mukden, Manchuria, in early November 1942. Mukden is located some few hundred miles south of Siberia and some close distance to Mongolia. The only things notable about Manchuria are that it is cold, cold, cold, and Elizabeth Taylor was never married there. The Manchurian men are tall, husky looking, and generally mustached. Cornmeal is one of the staples of their diet.

We were marched again, not too far, to an old, abandoned Chinese army barracks that must have been built when Confucius was still walking around. The old wooden barracks were halfway sunk into the earth, with only the tops of the barracks showing, probably as protection against the cold weather. They were dark and dreary looking. The wind whistled through the cracks in the barracks walls, making eerie and ominous sounds of welcome. We also found that there were other occupants of the barracks--huge, and I mean huge, ugly and hungry looking rats. *"Looks like good eatin's,"* someone said.

We were lined up and issued new prisoner identification numbers. As I approached the Jap issuing the numbers, he said *"Ju-san,"* which is 13 in Japanese. I jumped back and waved my hands in a "no" gesture. He looked startled, but before he could reply, the man who was in back of me, Lt. Mathews, stepped forward and said, *"I like that number, I'll take it."* So I became number 14 and I never thought I was superstitious. I am also happy that number 13, Lt. Mathews, survived.

At this time we were approximately 1,200 prisoners of war in this group from the original number of 2,000 who had left the Philippines (500 had been taken off the vessel at Kobe, Japan, and as I mentioned, our sick and dead had been taken ashore in Formosa).

49

The Japs lined us up and assigned us to various barracks and informed us that we would get one small bucket of coal a day for heating the barracks. We were happy to have the warm clothing they issued us in Korea.

They asked for the mess officer and I stepped forward. A surprisingly tall Jap officer motioned for me to follow him. He led me a few yards away to a small pile of rations on the ground, consisting of cornmeal, some cabbages, and about 40 lbs. of some kinds of meat. I stood as tall as I could (wishing I had my cowboy boots on) and said, *"This is all for 1,200 men?"* He angrily unsheathed his sword and shouted at me, *"You Americans are starving Japanese prisoners and also the Japanese you have imprisoned in the United States; you are also mistreating and killing them, we have this information from our newspapers. Japanese do not starve or kill their prisoners but treat them in accordance with our benevolent code of Bushido. This food is for the next three meals."*

During all this time he accented and punctuated his remarks by waving and thrusting his sword in my direction. I thought to myself, you and your big mouth are in trouble. However, I stood tall and said, *"This is not true. We also have a code of honor in our armies and in our government. Prisoners of war are fed the same rations issued to our troops and we further treat all prisoners strictly in accordance with the Geneva Convention, and our treatment of them is verified by the International Red Cross in Switzerland. If these prisoners are expected to work in your factories up here, they cannot subsist on these small rations."* Fortunately, I shut up after that. I was shaking a lot too. He glared at me, removed his sword in front of me, and sheathed it, to my relief. I was scared, but very angry too. I think, anger oftentimes gives you the incentive and courage to do things that you would not normally and rationally do. Anyway, I had told the son of a bitch off and felt good about it, and felt better about still being around.

Curiously, throughout the ensuing years I spent in this POW camp, this Jap officer became almost friendly to me. He would often give me a cigarette or two and even discussed the war with me. He was with us for about two years and then was transferred to the Russian front or what was to become the Russian front.

Above, General Wainwright forced to broadcast the surrender of the Philippines.

Left, Lieutenant General Masaharu Homma, Commander of the Japanese 14th Army. Tried and executed, by the Americans, April 3, 1946, for his responsibility for the Death March, and other atrocities. (National Archives)

December 17, 1984

Dear Mr. Bocksel:

My name on the return address on the envelope is not familiar to you at the moment. I hope that as I continue this letter to you, my name will become familiar to you again. To begin, I am a life member of The Defenders of Bataan & Corregidor and it was in the latest issue of the Quan that I saw your name and the death of your wife. Before I continue any further, may I extend to you my deepest sympathy on your loss. Now I would like to turn the clock back forty-one years. It was a cold winter day when we arrived in Mukden, Manchuria and that unpainted building in that first camp the Japs put us in. I had been a cook in the Navy and it was where we were in the building where the kitchen was that I saw one of the bravest acts I ever witnessed throughout the war and during our 3½ years of imprisonment. I was there when the Japanese Officers came with this small basket of meat which couldn't have weighed more than ten pounds and gave this ration of meat to you and said this was to feed the men in our camp. You looked at them eye-ball to eye-ball and said,"This is not near enough meat to feed all these men. They are weak, and sick from disease and hunger and must have more than this in order to survive." The officer in charge told you "This is more than you Americans are giving our people interned in your camps." It was then that you stood up to them and said, " That"s a damn lie and you know it." They could have killed you right then and there with one of the swords they all carried on their side. I was standing right beside you at that time and after all these years, I have never forgotten this act of courage. Many times I have told friends and relatives of A.A. Bocksel and his bravery.

At that time, I remembered you as being under six feet in height, and that you had a neatly trimmed moustache, dark in color and that you were a Junior Officer. Does my memory serve me correctly? I worked as a cook and a baker most of the 3½ years in both camps. I never knew if you had survived this ordeal and if you had made it back to the good old USA. Now I know you have after seeing this issue of the Quan. I wanted to write you this letter so you would know that you will never be forgotten as long as I live. We will probably never see each other again as we are both getting old. We are both so lucky to have lived all these years after what we went through. God Bless You Mr. Bocksel and with the approching holidays of Christmas and Chanukah may I extend my warmest, kindest and sincerest wishes to you.

Fraternally and sincerely,

Vernon K. Stroschein

Vernon K. Stroschein

Letter to Author from fellow POW Vernon Stroschein. 1984.

# 15

Cornmeal! Cornmeal! Cornmeal! Did you ever think you would hear a prisoner of war complain about food! While I respected the nutritive value and stomach filling qualities of cornmeal, I hated it--which undoubtedly reflected the fact that we were not starving at this time and had full stomachs. Twice a day. Cornmeal for breakfast and lunch and a watery soup for dinner. No salt, nothing on it. Apparently, it was an abundant crop in Manchuria and we were lucky to get it. Remember, not only Indians eat corn; northern Chinese and Prisoners of War do, too. If you should meet me in the morning, please don't ask me if I have had my cornmeal today, as is the custom among the Manchurians.

The Japs also added to our diet some form of Chinese barley they called "kaoliang." We used it in our supper meal, mixed with a few cabbage leaves or once in a great while some carrots or potatoes given to us as a treat. When the kaoliang was cooked, it turned a murky inky color, but it was good food. The small ration of meat given to us was always chopped up and put in the soup. We tried everything to make the cornmeal more palatable; importuned the Japs for more salt rations; tried baking it, and finally saturated it with garlic. About the garlic: I was speaking to the Jap Mess Officer in charge of rations and had just finished a request for more salt and was asking for any other type of seasoning we might obtain for the cornmeal. He mentioned that they might be able to get some garlic for us as the Chinese used copious amounts. Sure enough, some weeks later a trailer truck pulled into the prison compound and dropped tons of garlic. Cornmeal with garlic became an epicurean dish. The men also roasted the garlic and ate it like peanuts. For a while, even the Japs stayed away from the compound.

I would reiterate again at this time that the mere fact that we were complaining about the taste of the food indicates that we were being fed better and getting physically stronger. I honestly believe, as prison camps go, that we were in a better one than most. Mortality rates had fallen drastically and I recall that we had only lost about 200 men out of this group. Another favorable factor was that the men who worked in the factory were fed lunch there, and their fare was a little better than what the prison camp provided.

About seven months later, we had to pack up again and were moved to a new camp in Mukden, Manchuria. It was nearby, so the march was easy this time. The camp was located next to a factory where our men were to work. To my knowledge, no one was beaten or abused during this march.

The barracks were new, two stories high and consisted of about ten structures. The compound was surrounded by an eight foot high brick wall, topped with electrically charged barbed wire. The perimeter was constantly patrolled by Jap guards. Upon entering the complex, I did not realize that I would spend almost three years here and during this time would not see trees, grass, shrubs, and the countryside.

## 16

At this time, I guess, I should tell you about my close friend and prison buddy, Dan.

Dan McCartney, 200th Coast Artillery, from Deming, New Mexico. As a state, New Mexico had the largest number of men in the Bataan-Corregidor saga. They were a National Guard unit that was activated in the early part of 1941. I sailed over with them, though I was not assigned to this unit.

I became friendly with Dan on the trip. We went ashore together in Hawaii and had a great time. After we parted in Manila, we did not meet again until we found ourselves in Cabanatuan prison camp. Dan also had made the Bataan Death March and had survived the infamous Camp O'Donnell prison camp.

When the group of men to go to Manchuria was selected by the Japs, Dan and I were among them. We were happy to be with each other again. For the next three years, we slept next to each other, shared any extra food we stole from the Japs, took care of each other when sick, commiserated together, and had a lot of laughs together. We were as close as any two brothers could be. I loved him as a brother.

He used to say, *"If we don't make it, we won't have to worry about it any more."* Dan survived prison camp with me. We just hugged and hugged each other with tears in our eyes when the Russians liberated us. We saw each other continually throughout the years after we returned home, for over 40 years.  He died in 1986, undoubtedly from the residual effects of 3-1/2 years of Japanese treatment in prison camp.  I still miss him so much...and Dan, don't forget to save the bunk next to you for me, when I join you.

Author, right, with Dan McCartney in Mukden POW Camp, one month after liberation.

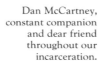

Dan McCartney, constant companion and dear friend throughout our incarceration.

## 17

Soon after we arrived in the new camp in Manchuria, we were joined by a small contingent of British and Australian troops from Singapore, about 100 men. We related favorably during our three years together. I made another close friend among them, Captain James Johnson. Johnny was a Sandhurst man; warm, friendly, witty, and fun to be with--even in a prison camp. He was an amateur philologist and was always telling us the derivation of words, like "salary" is derived from the word "*salarium*," meaning salt money. Thus the expression "to earn one's salt." I often told Johnny that I was not particularly interested in improving my education at this time. Johnny survived too. We visited each other in London and New York several times in later years, and corresponded with each other for over 40 years, until his death in 1986. Close friend and good buddy.

From my Australian prison mates I learned some of the most descriptive words in the Australian they spoke. Take an expression like "absolutely beautiful." They would say "*absofuckinglutely beautiful*"; or "*absofuckinglutely awful,*" etc. Even though this language may be offensive, I find that I am absofuckinglutely unable to delete it!

The men in our camp were working in a nearby factory. This was in accord with the Geneva Convention. Officers, however, were not required to work for the enemy while prisoners of war, in accord with the provisions of the Geneva Convention. Ever since we were captured, the Japs disregarded these regulations requiring officers to work in any capacity they dictated. (An interesting note about the factory was that it was designed by American Engineers in 1940. It was called the M.K.K. factory, and was situated in close proximity to our prison camp.)

Major Hankins, our commanding officer, requested a meeting with the Jap commander, Colonel Matsuda, in this regard. Hank advised the Jap Colonel that captured officers could not work for the enemy and further their war effort. He said he and the officers in camp would assume any duties assigned that were related to the care and welfare of their men. He said that the Colonel as a career military man should understand our position, etc.

Hank did it! The Colonel relented and the officers in the camp were assigned duties only related to the wellbeing of our men. This was just after the Battle of Midway, in which the Japanese Navy was severely beaten. Maybe the Colonel saw the "handwriting on the wall," or may be he was not such a bad guy.

I was still assigned mess officer of the camp at this time, early 1943. While we were given enough cornmeal and kaoliang (barley) to eat, it was not enough nutritionally to stave off the ravages of beriberi, scurvy, pellagra, and other vitamin deficient diseases. However, we were in better condition than at the time of our earlier prison days. Men were starting to weigh approximately from 100 to 130 lbs. on the average. The men in our "hospital," however, were still in deplorable condition. Men lay on straw pallets fighting their last battle, at least most of them, in an area assigned as the "hospital." Bad as our conditions were, they were much worse in other prison camps, especially in Japan, where prisoners worked in coal and copper mines under extremely bad conditions.

I would note again that out of approximately 24,000 to 25,000 American POWs, only 9,700 survived. It has not been possible to establish with any accuracy the numbers of Filipinos who perished while in Jap custody, but the number has been estimated as high as 30,000 to 40,000.

The Veterans Administration released a study in 1983, which determined that the most inhuman treatment ever afforded prisoners of war was by the Japanese in WW II and the Koreans during the Korean conflict.

I feel that all of our prisoners of war, regardless who their captors were, suffered the same mental anguish, the same loss of freedom, and the same degrees of humiliation and deprivation that men endure under these circumstances.

Under most inhuman treatment I would also place at the top of the list those American prisoners of war captured during the Viet Nam war.

First letter sent home after more than two years as a POW.

Infamous Corporal Noda. Interpretor at Mukden POW Camp. Sentenced to 20 years imprisonment, released after 7 years.

"The Bull", most cruel of Japanese at Mukden. Reportedly killed.

Capt. Murate, Jap Doctor. Hanged for mistreatment of POW's.

# 18

Around this time the Vatican was able to effect a monetary donation for the welfare of the POWs. I believe, our allocation was several hundred dollars. Major Hankins requested that medicines be purchased with the money. He was told that this was impossible, didn't we know that there was a war still going on and that medicines were in very short supply? etc. They went on to say that when medicines were available, they would be furnished to POWs (like charcoal for dysentery or Jap tooth powder for stomach ailments). Incidentally, the tooth powder, apart from its use as a seasoning for cornmeal by some of the men, did actually have some beneficial effect on minor stomach problems--probably a psychosomatic effect.

The end result was that they purchased musical instruments with the money. It fed the soul, anyhow, and actually turned out to be a great morale builder as we were allowed to form a small band for entertainment purposes. I learned to play the Hawaiian guitar, eventually proficient enough to become a member of the band, *The Mukden Snowballs*. About the same time, we also received some reading material from the Salvation Army. They were a God-send, as we had nothing to read prior to this time.

It was common for us to read the same book over and over. Interestingly, I read a romantic novel while there, and the name of the heroine was "Merrie." I liked the name so much that I said to Dan one day that if I ever lived through this mess and returned home and married some girl and we had children, if we had a girl I was going to name her "Merrie." Well, I got home, married, had a daughter, and her name is "Merrie."

One of the guards and interpreters was a Jap named Corporal Noda. He had attended schools in Berkeley, California, and was studying in Japan at the commencement of hostilities. He was conscripted into the Japanese Army and because of his knowledge of Americans and the English language, was assigned to our prison camp. He hated Americans and was responsible for much of our misery. We called him "The Rat"; his favorite punishment of us, apart from slaps and blows, was to have a prisoner run around the compound until he dropped from exhaustion.

Noda hated me personally because of an incident that occurred while I was mess officer. He came into our barracks one evening in an ostensibly affable mood, reminiscing about Americana--hot dogs, hamburgers, milkshakes, Yankees, Dodgers, etc. He suddenly turned to me and said, *"Bocksel, how about getting some meat from the kitchen and having one of the cooks fix me a good stateside burger."* I looked at him in amazement and replied that this was the first meat ration we had received in over two weeks time, and to do that would deprive about 20 men of their meat ration the next day. He looked at me in amazement and anger and stormed out of the barracks.

After that he made my life hell, with his hatred and abuse. He had me removed as mess officer and I was assigned to other duties in the camp. He retained his enmity towards me until the day he was transferred out of the POW camp. The son of a bitch, asking me to get him a hamburger!

He was a common object of loathing.

After the war, at the War Crimes Trials, Colonel Matsuda was hanged; one of the doctors, Lieutenant Murata, was also hanged, Corporal Noda was sentenced to 20 years imprisonment. My friend, Dan testified at the War

Crimes Trials.

Dan brought me back a photograph of Noda in his prison garb, which I have kept to this day as a reminder of evil. Some years later I learned that he was released after seven years imprisonment. I hope he is not back in California running a Jap restaurant.

Another mean, sadistic, and ugly bastard among our captors was a Captain Ishikawa. He was second in command of the prison camp. About 5 feet tall and 3 feet wide, he weighed in at well over 250 lbs. For an infraction or imagined infraction of their rules, he would beat the hell out of you. He was a genuine "Samurai," he never beat anyone to death, just close to it. We called him "The Bull," because he was mean and sadistic.

He gave me the worst beating I experienced as a POW. He came into our barracks late one evening, and as required, we all jumped to "Attention" and bowed low, from the waist. I apparently was the last person to stand up. He screamed for me to step forward, which I did, and then proceeded to punch me repeatedly in the face, stomach, and back, knocking me to the ground with almost every blow. I lay on the ground and he hit me with his sword, fortunately still in its scabbard. I felt piercing pains and tasted blood and pieces of teeth in my mouth. One of the Jap interpreters who accompanied him, whispered to me to stand up after he hit me each time or he would probably beat me to death. (The name of this interpreter was Kawashima. He had spent some years in Hawaii and in his compassion tried to help the prisoners whenever he could. However, he was only a private and not very influential with his peers.) The Bull kept pummeling me and I would stagger up after each blow, for how long, I don't know. He ended with a long tirade after he finished with me--in Japanese, so I don't know what he said. After he left, I called him some choice names I can't repeat now. I was bruised, black and blue, and crippled for a long time afterwards.

61

Many others in our group could tell you similar stories about their encounters with the Bull, especially Derrick Barton. One day he beat up Bart for some minor infraction (like breathing too loud or something of that nature). He started beating Bart at the top of a stairway and mercilessly beat him all the way to the bottom of this long staircase. He left him practically unconscious. Bart was a long time recuperating. Any time Bart and I meet again, we reminisce about our beatings from the Bull. I am still constantly reminded of it from the many back problems I have to this day. Beatings from the Japs were a degrading and humiliating experience. The only defense we had was the will to survive, when all the odds were against survival. I feel that all prisoners who were abused and beaten exhibited a particular part of valor; that of their determination to absorb the cruel treatment, without begging for mercy.

The Bull was, fortunately, transferred to the Manchurian border to fight the Russians when they came. We heard that he was killed up there. It couldn't have happened to a "nicer" guy. I believe if he and Noda had been in our prison camp at the time of our liberation, they would have been in serious jeopardy. One of us would surely have killed them.

Colonel Matsuda, the Jap commander of our prisoner of war camp, was hanged after the war. I personally felt the punishment was too severe in his case. Especially when Cpl. Noda was sentenced to 20 years in prison and released after serving only 7 years. I never saw Colonel Matsuda ever strike a prisoner, nor anyone else in our group. True, he was in charge of the camp, and our lack of food, medicines, and mistreatment were attributed to his management of the camp, but he was a career soldier and surely implemented only the policies regarding treatment of prisoners of war dictated by the high command in Tokyo. My personal observation and opinion were that he was a compassionate man who was honestly distressed by the plight of the prisoners. I think his crimes were in not supervising his staff closely, especially Japs like Noda, The Bull, the camp doctor, Murata, and others.

I remember, one day, when I was quite ill, Colonel Matsuda passed by me and through his interpreter inquired as to my condition. Before he left, he patted my cheek in a kindly gesture and said through his interpreter that he hoped I would recover and return home to my family one day. Had I been able to attend the War Crimes Trials in Tokyo after the war, I would have spoken on his behalf.

Colonel Matsuda was also instrumental in obtaining approval for the issuance of soybeans, as a supplement to our basic cornmeal and kaoliang diet.

While I was mess officer, I remembered reading somewhere about the nutritive value of soybeans. It was primarily used as a feed for livestock and had many other uses. I also learned that it was one of the principal crops in Manchuria. I discussed this with our commanding officer, Major Hankins, and our doctors. They were enthusiastic about it and the major said he would discuss it with Colonel Matsuda at the next opportunity. I should note that soybeans are extremely high in protein, which was sorely missing in our diet.

When Hankins was finally able to see the Jap Colonel, Matsuda said that soybeans were not edible by humans and used chiefly as cattle fodder.

Hankins persisted, and Matsuda finally agreed to get permission to obtain a sack of soybeans for trial. When they finally arrived, they were turned over to me as mess officer. Fortunately, we had as mess sergeant an older man, Andy Prevusnak, who was born in Czechoslovakia and after coming to the U.S. had joined the Army. At that time he had been an Army cook for over 15 years. Andy soaked the soybeans for about 10 hours before cooking them. They were still hard as rocks and the men who ate them had severe stomach cramps and more diarrhea--which they needed like a hole in the head. Someone said, *"Jesus, I hope they never give us chocolate, it would probably be Ex-Lax."*

Old Andy persisted and said, *"I can cook these Goddamn beans, if it is the last thing I ever do."* We experimented, and finally found the formula. Soak the beans for 48 hours and then cook them for 10 hours or so. We added them to the soup at night and the men liked them. Later on, when we were moved to the new camp in Mukden, Andy made a mash of them after they were cooked and baked them in an oven. What came out was palatable and, more importantly, nourishing. It became a great adjunct to our diet and its influence on the men's health was evidenced some months later.

To my knowledge, we were the only Japanese POW camp to get soybeans as a portion of our ration, and we owe thanks to Andy for making it a reality.

Even today, at our National Conventions, someone who had been in Mukden will come up to me and say, *"Boxie, if it weren't for those soybeans, a lot of us would not be here today."* Someone else chimes in, *"Don't forget about the dogs,"* so I will tell you about the dogs.

When we first arrived in Manchuria and located in the old Chinese barracks, we were in a large and open area surrounded by barbed wire. In Manchuria, at that time, wild dogs ran in huge packs throughout the countryside, scavenging food anywhere. They were dangerous, too.

One day, a large pack of dogs ran into camp and received quite a surprise. Our men attacked them with sticks, stones, and anything else they could lay their hands on as weapons. Some got away, but a lot of them didn't, and many of us had fresh meat again. Let me assure you that dog meat is mouth watering and delicious if you are hungry, even if it is a little tough to chew. A nice lean dog chop, rubbed with a little garlic, was a gourmet's delight.

Makes me salivate, just thinking about it. The men made mittens of the fur, too.

The dogs came back a few more times to our delight. But, like all good things, it ended; they finally ceased coming. While this was going on, the Japs just laughed at us.

Dog meat is no different than eating wild rabbit, possum, or squirrel. And cats have always been a delicacy to the Chinese. And how about those Texans, eating rattlesnakes!

The only thing I could never eat was monkey. One time, while I was on Bataan, someone cooked a monkey. I believe it was a Filipino who roasted it over a fire after skinning it. When finished it looked like a frightened baby burned to death in the fetal position.

Some years after the war I was reading a story about the Eskimos. There was an interesting piece in it, describing how the Eskimos killed wolves. They would chop a hole in the ice and place a knife handle in the hole. When it froze and was rigid, they would rub the blood of seals around the blade of the knife. When the wolves came and smelled the blood, they would lick the blade of the knife, effectively ex-sanguinating themselves. Wish I had known this in Manchuria!

# 19

In Cabanatuan prison camp, I once heard a very eloquent prayer by one of the prisoners. He didn't know or care if anyone was listening. He had severe dysentery, was dehydrated, with a gunny sack around his legs and stomach, couldn't have weighed more than 70 lbs., soaking wet and lying on the ground in close proximity to the latrine, which he apparently couldn't make. His eyes were glaring and fixed, staring up. I heard him say in a cracked, pleading voice, *"God, where the fuck are you?"* In his pain and confusion he was praying and reaching out to God.

I understand his feelings and his eloquent prayer. We had a Catholic chaplain on Bataan who said, *"There are no atheists in fox-holes."* His words have become world famous. Yes, I doubt strongly that there were any among us. Perhaps agnostics, but not atheists. However, there were a lot among us who had felt that religion was like an umbrella--only to be opened when it rained.

My own religious beliefs were shaken when I was captured. While I still believed and prayed, I could not understand or accept the things I had witnessed and been through. Millions of people throughout the world were praying for God to stop the war. Why didn't He interfere and stop it, through his miraculous powers; why was He allowing it to go on with the horrible carnage inflicted on so many millions, around me and on countless other war-torn countries? Why? Why? Why?

Through meditation and prayer I found some of the

answers to my dilemma. God doesn't cause wars. Men do. God in His love for us weeps for us during these times. Man, with his selfishness, greed, and hate, causes wars. God does not intervene because He gave us free will to make our own choices. Man is the culprit. God loves all of us with the same fervor and intensity with which we love our children, parents, or mates. We know this because we are made in the image and likeness of God and He gave us these inherent instincts to love our loved ones with indescribable intensity. He wants us to love one another in the same way. He said it, *"Love one another, as I love you."*

If we weep, we know He has wept--many times throughout the history of mankind.

Christ said, *"Unless you be as little children, ye shall not enter the Kingdom of Heaven."* To be as little children means to bow down your intellect and believe. What always surprises me is that people will accept and believe historically recorded facts, such as Hannibal crossing the Alps; the exploits of Napoleon; the story of Genghis Khan; and countless other historical facts of other figures and events. However, when it comes to accepting the historical events recorded in the New Testament, many have difficulties accepting these writings.

A theologian once said, *"Christ was either the Son of God or the greatest phoney ever perpetrated on the world. A phoney cannot endure for 2,000 years."*

(I have been referring primarily to the Christian ethic in these remarks; however, I have the deepest respect for all religions of this world and know that people of all religions find comfort and solace in their religious beliefs.)

Someone explained it better than I can: "Imagine a mountain, the top of which is God, with many different paths from the bottom to the top. Some are straight; some are narrow; some are winding; some are more difficult to tread; but they all lead to the top, if you only mount upwards.

# 20

We were beginning our third year of confinement. The roar of death had fallen to a whisper. Basically, the stronger had survived. It was a surprising fact to me that so many, many of the very young men in our midst had died. The ratio of death among the young was measurably higher than death among the older prisoners. By young, I mean those men in the 18-22 age bracket. I felt the toll was higher among them because they lacked some of the resourcefulness, experience, wisdom, and will that more mature men acquire through experience.

In Mukden, we had a problem with burials in the winter months. The ground would freeze to a depth of 3-4 feet ard it was impossible during this period to dig graves with the implements available to us. Consequently, anyone who died during the winter months, was placed in a large shed in the prison compound. One body stacked upon the other, waiting for the thaw which generally came around the month of May. As the thawing weather approached, the stench emanating from the shed was awful. I must say that Colonel Matsuda allowed us to bury each man in one grave and to place simple wooden crosses or other religious symbols on each grave. This was another of his kind gestures to us.

One wonderful day, the Japs gave us censored mail from home--one letter. I learned from my family that they had only been advised six months previously that I was a POW--more than two years after my capture. Families of

POWs and of those missing in action also suffer during a war, and endure anguish over not knowing the fate of their loved ones. We were informed by the Japs that we might send a 50 word message home, censored by them. One man wrote, "...*and I am well, and the food is good. Tell all my friends, especially tell it to the Marines.*" The Jap interpreters, who censored the mail, were apparently not aware of the colloquialism "tell it to the Marines" (old British Navy slang for explanation of disbelief).

In this, the beginning of our third year in captivity, or, as some of us used to say, "our barbed wire rendezvous," we were fed enough cornmeal, barley, and soybeans to sustain life. I should mention that we were also given a small piece of bread once a day. Medicines were still lacking, but fortunately, our death rate was very low. The problems we experienced with flies in the Philippines were almost non-existent in the colder climate we were now in.

The pangs of hunger were always with us, even after two bowls of cornmeal. We missed American food. We would sit around for hours and hours, and talk about nothing but food. A form of mental masturbation. We would tell about the best hamburger, steak, pie and chicken we had eaten. Someone would say, *"My mother makes the best biscuits smothered in chicken gravy, with Southern fried chicken...My mother makes the best spaghetti sauce, smothered in mushrooms...My wife makes the best roast beef with Yorkshire pudding...."* Dan says, *"I have to leave, I have indigestion."* We all laugh.

Then someone talks about desserts and other sweets. We start by talking about cakes, pies, chocolate, and puddings. We start a list of all of them with vivid descriptions of how they were made and how they tasted. We ended up with hundreds of recipes, savoring each one.

When I fell asleep that night, I found myself having dinner with the guy's mother who makes the chicken and biscuits. He was right, it was absolutely divine, especially the way she served it. She brought steaming platters of food to the table, filled each plate with loads of chicken; steaming mashed potatoes, drowned in gravy; hot, fluffy white biscuits; peas, swimming in butter, and gallons of milk. I had three helpings, topped off with hot apple pie swimming in ice cream. (Now you know why we hated to wake up sometimes.)

Sleep is the opiate of those imprisoned. With eyes closed in slumber, you re-enter old worlds and familiar places. You can go back home and visit with your family and friends again. Eat another of Mom's great meals, see close friends, especially old girlfriends, have fun, and most of all, escape from the reality which is now. Sleep greatly helps time pass, too. The Japs constantly patrol our barracks and allow us only to sleep at night, causing me to miss many reunions with my family.

* * * * * * * *

I have been frequently asked if we missed women during our years of captivity. Sure we missed women-- mothers, sisters, wives, daughters. Yes, we sure did miss them.

But that really is not what they meant when asking the question. They were referring to sex, and the answer is NO. Hungry, sick, starving, and surviving men do not think about sex. You only miss food and water when you don't get it, not sex. We were Barbed Wire Celibates, with no problem in this regard.

The self-preservation and hunger instincts take infinitely greater precedence over the sexual instinct. Sorry girls, we only pursue you when we are well fed and contented. As I have mentioned previously in this narrative, before the war I thought a siren was a blonde, until I learned it was an air raid alarm.

I must confess, though, that I did have a girlfriend in

prison camp. No one else ever knew it or found out about it. She would secretly visit me, but only at night when everyone was asleep. She was very beautiful and always dressed in blue. Strangely though, she never spoke a word, but she loved me and comforted me each time she came. I never found out what her last name was, but I knew her first name, it was Mary, and she told me that she had a son who was persecuted too, many years ago. She mentioned he was born in Bethlehem.

(National Archives)
General McArthur embracing General Wainwright after his release from a Japanese Prison Camp.

71

# 21

As I have mentioned, I was in a group of 16 officers assigned to this prison camp. We lived together in great harmony despite the eccentricities we all displayed at times, often magnified by circumstances. After three years of living closely together, there was a lot of love among us, some dislikes, but no hatred. I have already written about Dan McCartney, my closest friend and prison mate. Another great friend was Al Wheeler. Tall, ruggedly handsome, kind and generous, Al was quite an unusual person in his accomplishments. University graduate, cow puncher, ex-professional boxer, gold prospector, linguist, and ex- hobo. Above all, he was a sincere and gentle person. He was the first among us to learn to speak Japanese fluently. To me he was a tower of strength and inspiration during those times.

After the American forces had retaken the Philippines and were preparing for the invasion of Japan, we heard a rumor in the camp that the Japs were going to move us to another prison camp, either further north in Manchuria or to Japan proper. Al, Dan, and I vowed that if they were going to put us on another train, ship, or railway car, we were going to attempt escape. We had a steel file that was honed into a knife-like weapon, and a good cache of cornmeal and barley for food. The weather was turning warmer in Manchuria and we hoped that if we successfully escaped, we might encounter some friendly Manchurians, who would assist us. (The Manchurians hated their Japanese conquerors.) Some few weeks prior to our liberation, the rumors were strong that they were going to move us to a new location. The rumors were reinforced this time by the fact that the Japs were making rice balls; which generally was the food they gave us for "traveling." Their plans never materialized as the war ended a few weeks later as a result of the atomic bomb and we did not have to pursue our "escape plans."

Al Wheeler stayed on in the service after we returned home. He fought again in the Korean War and lost one of his eyes in that encounter. He was featured in *LIFE* Magazine in one of their stories on the Korean War, wearing a black patch over his eye.

He was retired from the Army as a result of his injuries in WWII and the Korean War. With the black eye patch he wore, he looked like the prototype of a typical soldier of fortune. Unfortunately, some few years later he was killed, when a bus he was riding in Mexico skidded and ran over a cliff in a severe rainstorm. I shall always treasure the memory of him.

Another close friend of mine was Lt. Elmer Shabart, M.D. and Surgeon and one of the best. Under practically primitive medical conditions he removed gangrenous legs and arms when all other prison camp treatment failed. He performed all other major surgical procedures in the prison camp and was ingenious in his makeshift methods. He also saved my life. Along with all the other sickness and diseases I had in early 1943, I came down with a severe case of hepatitis, serious infection of the liver. For several months I was in agonizing pain every single day; the kind of pain where you don't care whether you live or not. But for some reason I still did not want to go to the "hospital," and thanks to Elmer I remained in the barracks. He was trying desperately to get me some suitable medicine from the Japs, and finally succeeded. The medicine was called *"Duma,"* and it eventually cured me.

73

I helped Elmer at times in the hospital, which is why I suppose my grandchildren call me "Horse Doctor" today.

He retired as Chief of Thoracic Surgery for the Veterans Administration and is presently living in California. We visited each other once since the war but have faithfully corresponded with each other throughout the intervening years. I still owe you a "big one," Elmer.

Dr. Mark Herbst was another fine doctor in our group who kept meticulous medical records on every prisoner, which proved invaluable in later years for claims of ex-prisoners with the Veterans Administration.

Others in this close-knit group of men who I have not previously mentioned, were: Jack Rogers, Bucky Walters, Bill Moseman, Don Thompson, Boyd Hanson, Carl Weeks, Jake Levie, Thurman Matthews, and Neville Grow. They will always be in my memories.

Author, right, with Bucky Walters in Mukden POW Barracks, one month after liberation. Sept. 1945.

Boyd Hansen, Jack Rogers & Don Thompson. 1946.   Al Wheeler & Author (right). 1947.

Author and some of his fellow POW's from Mukden Camp, after liberation.

# 22

Early 1945 saw our condition improving a bit. We were given a little fish or meat once or twice a week, a small piece of bread each day, and our mess sergeant, Andy, concocted "coffee" for us in the mornings. He took the kaoliang (barley) and roasted the kernels in a pan, until they were browned, added water, and presto, coffee! It actually tasted good. Now, if we only could get some orange juice....

Maybe the Japs knew they were losing the war, or maybe it was a kind gesture from Colonel Matsuda.

We learned later that our forces were advancing closer to Japan, having secured the Philippines. At the time, or I should say, throughout our entire imprisonment, we never actually knew the progress of the war, as we had no communication with the outside world whatsoever..

One day, the Japs brought in a load of baby chicks, perhaps a hundred or so. They wanted two officers to take care of them (we later learned, for their propaganda purposes). I was selected by Major Hankins, as was my good friend Captain Johnson of the British contingent. What a selection! I, from Brooklyn, and Johnny from the heart of London. Some chicken farmers! Neither of us had ever seen a chicken, except on a plate. We built a chicken coop and actually learned to raise chicken from some farm boys in our midst.

Some weeks later, the Japs came with cameras and filmed us tending the chicken. Propaganda, no doubt, for their news reels, depicting their kindness to their prisoners. The film, I am sure, did not mention that we were told that the eggs were for the Japanese mess and that they never gave a single egg to the prisoners.

Well, the day finally arrived when the chicken which had survived became young ladies and started laying eggs. To be sure, Johnny and I had a few raw samples. In good conscience we decided that we would give the eggs we stole to our doctors for their distribution among the most needy cases in the hospital. We started with a few eggs a day, but suddenly our "crop" mushroomed to 20-30 eggs a day, all of which we gave to the hospital--almost all.

One sunny day, storm clouds appeared, and the "bubble" burst. The goddamned chicken, like all women, couldn't keep their mouths shut. Every time one of them laid an egg, you could hear the cackling all over the compound. Johnny said, *"Christ, you would think they were laying square eggs, with all the noise they are making."* I said, *"You would be screaming too, if you were a chicken laying square eggs."*

Sure enough, their symphonic sounds reached the Japs' ears and one of the Jap officers came over to us and inquired if the chicken had started laying eggs. Yes, we said, just today, two eggs (called *tomago* by them). He grinned, took the two eggs and returned a short time later with several more Japs. To our sheer horror, they took a long chain and lock and locked the hen house door shut, saying they would return tomorrow to collect the eggs.

We were dumbfounded and scared, too. What in the hell was going to happen to us tomorrow when they came and found 20-30 eggs? Johnny, who was a devout Catholic, joined me in a corner of the coop where we made a novena of sorts, promising to give up women and liquor forever if we ever got out of this place alive.

We were in serious trouble, because stealing is a major offense in the Japanese military code. Many times

76

throughout our incarceration, the Japanese colonel would admonish us about stealing and telling lies, and the severe punishment meted out by them for these offenses.

Excerpts from one of his many addresses to us on this subject (translation into English by one of his interpreters):

*It has come to my attention that some of you prisoners have been steal and tell lies. The Japanese soldier will never be steal or tell lies because of honor in our code of Bushido. If we detection any prisoner who will be steal or tell lies, we will punish her very severely. We will be to kill him dead.*

Johnny and I didn't sleep that night, we were praying all night. The next morning we went over to the chicken coop and looked through the window and I said, *"Oh my God,"* and almost fainted. Johnny took another look and did. The coop was full of eggs. We had about two hours time before the Japs were due over at noon. Two hours to "E" day (Egg Day).

I said to Johnny that we had to try and get the eggs out some way because if we didn't, or were caught trying to get them, we would be in trouble. I said that I would attempt to get into the coop by prying the window open and while I was doing this, he should rake and sweep, raising as much dust as he could. When I got inside the coop, I'd pass him the eggs as fast as I could. *"Right-o,"* said Johnny, and I said, *"I'm glad you didn't say 'Cheerio, my dear Watson.'"*

Johnny proceeded to make a lot of dust and I, with my hands behind me, worked on getting the window loose. To my utter amazement, I found the window pane loose. Somebody up there liked us or the Novena had paid off. With cut, bleeding fingers, I got the glass off and crawled through the opening in about 1/2 second flat, scared the chickens to death, and passed the eggs out to Johnny, who stuffed them inside his tunic. I believe I can claim a Ripley's Believe It or Not: about 30 eggs tossed out in about 3 seconds. I left three eggs in the nests, crawled out the window again, replaced the window pane, and almost hugged Johnny--when I remembered the eggs in his shirt. We did it, we did it!

Around 12 o'clock noon, the Japs came, four of them, including Colonel Matsuda. They were laughing and jabbering as they ceremoniously unlocked the door of the hen house. A little Jap went in and came out with four eggs (some bitch of a chicken had laid another egg). The Japs appeared surprised and jabbered among themselves again, but did not say a word to us. They locked the hen house door again and said *"Ashta"* to us, which means "tomorrow" in Japanese and "curtains" for us. We got away with it today, but knew we would never get away with it again.

All of a sudden, I see Johnny spring to attention and approach Colonel Matsuda. Saluting him in the smart manner that only the British can do, he says, *"Sir, I am a graduate of Sandhurst, and brought up in the same military traditions as you. I am an officer of His Majesty King George's Military forces and like you, I am an officer and a gentleman. I consider locking this door as an act impugning upon my integrity and honor. Further, how can we clean the hen house and feed the chicken if the door is locked? I ask you to reconsider this action. Thank you.*

He saluted the Colonel again, smartly as ever, and stepped back. I said to myself, this crazy Limey has got us both killed now for sure. The Jap interpreter was translating to the Colonel as Johnny spoke. The Colonel mused for a while and then spoke to his aides and the next thing we knew, they were unlocking the door, taking the lock and chain with them. The Colonel looked at both of us as he left and while he didn't smile, there was a benign look on his face. Suddenly, it was miraculously over. We couldn't believe it.

I said a "Hail Mary" and I know Johnny did too. He had a smirk on his face when he looked at me, that said, what did you think of my show? I hugged him and said: *"I thought you were going to get us killed by beheading or getting shot at sunrise; and this crazy Limey I am mixed up is really crazy--but I love you."* And we laughed and laughed to such a point that we should have wet our pants...I don't know about Johnny, but I had already done so.

Each day thereafter we increased the number of eggs we gave the Japs until we were giving them about 90% of the eggs laid. The rest we still sneaked to the hospital and once in a while, when our conscience would allow, we treated ourselves to one. I think we deserved it.

I've often wondered about the Jap capitulation in this incident. Was it Johnny's superb performance; were the Japs afraid of "losing face"; or was the Colonel just a "good guy"?

Col. Johnny Johnson,
British Loyals Regiment.
Dear friend and
"Commandant"
of the "Chicken Coop".

## 23

One day, during 1944, we were addressed by the Jap colonel on the virtues of the benevolent Japanese. At the conclusion of his address, he announced that they had received American Red Cross packages for us via the Red Cross in Switzerland. We could hardly believe the news. A dream come true. The packages were issued to us and Major Hankins called a meeting of the American, British, and Australian officers and men. He wisely suggested that rather than issue each man a package of food individually, we retain all of the food in a small warehouse and issue one item of food to each man, every day. The British and Australians opted for the complete package of food to be issued to each man, so Hank turned over their packages to them. He presented strong, sensible reasons for his suggestion and almost every American was in agreement. He further stated that this arrangement would prevent stealing from each other and provide nutrition over a longer period of time. He continued, the average prisoner, himself included, would probably consume this food ravenously in a very short time, with possible adverse effects from the radical change in our diet.

That day he issued one tin of corned beef for each two men. Talk about filet mignon or prime rib--this was better. Each mouthful was savored. A jubilant ambience permeated the atmosphere. Hate had a birthday.

Among the items I recall in the food packages were canned butter, of which you would place a small amount on your tongue and savor every drop as it melted; then there were raisins, cookies, canned biscuits, cigarettes, prunes, vitamins, some army rations, toothbrushes, toothpaste, jelly, canned fruit, cheese, cocoa, chocolate, and jam.

Every item was a gastronomical delight often consumed with tears in your eyes. I think, the tears were because the food was gone. Thanks to Hank's ingenuity, the food lasted for several months. It was a cafeteria of hope and joy to know that we were not forgotten.

We later learned that the food had been in the Jap warehouse for many months prior to its issue to us. Some more Bushido, I guess.

We only received one package of food throughout our imprisonment.

Part of the cemetery at Mukden, Manchuria. Flag raised after liberation.

# 24

One day, three men escaped from Mukden. They were, unfortunately, caught about a week later and returned to the prison camp. The Japs said that they had murdered a Manchurian policeman in their escape and would be executed for this. They were all very young and were executed by a firing squad. (This incident may have been one of the prime considerations by the War Crimes Tribunal in executing Colonel Matsudo.)

At about this time (late 1944), unknown to us, the American forces under General McArthur were preparing for the invasion of the Philippines. The Navy was strongly for bypassing the Philippines, in the same island hopping strategy that had proven so successful in the Pacific. However, McArthur's plan, with approval of President Roosevelt, prevailed.

Apart from strategic considerations by McArthur, he was undoubtedly influenced by his promise to the Filipinos of "I shall return." It was their great rallying cry.

Our Navy's devastating defeat of the Japanese Navy at Midway had dealt Japan a death blow and the brilliant island hopping strategy of our forces in the Pacific had speeded up our timetable for the recapture of the Philippines and for McArthur's return.

In late October, 1944, General McArthur waded ashore on the beach in Leyte Gulf in the Philippines. He had returned. A broadcasting unit was set up and he spoke:

*People of the Philippines, I have returned. By the grace of the Almighty God, our forces stand on Philippine soil--soil consecrated in the blood of our two peoples. We have come dedicated and committed to the task of destroying every vestige of enemy control over your daily lives, and of restoring the liberties of your people upon a foundation of indestructible strength.*

*At my side is your President, Sergio Osmena, a worthy successor of that great patriot, Manuel Quezon, with members of his cabinet. The seat of your government is now, therefore, firmly reestablished on Philippine soil.*

*The hour of your redemption is here. Your patriots have demonstrated an unswerving and resolute devotion to the principles of freedom that challenge the best that is written on the pages of human history. I now call upon your supreme effort that the enemy may know, from the temper of an aroused people within, that he has a force there to contend with no less violent than is the force committed from without.*

*Rally to me. Let the indomitable spirit of Bataan and Corregidor lead on. As the lines of battle roll forward to bring you within the zones of operation, rise and strike! Strike at every favorable opportunity. For your homes and hearths, strike! For future generations of your sons and daughters, strike! In the name of your sacred dead, strike! Let no heart be faint. Let every arm be steeled. The guidance of the Divine God points the way. Follow in his name to the Holy Grail of righteous victory.*

# 25

Some short time prior to this, the Japanese were evacuating most of the remaining prisoners in the Philippines to Japan, to prevent their liberation by the American forces. These men were loaded on unmarked Japanese vessels. They were in poor physical condition from the ravages of the Japanese internment. Many were walking cadavers who were packed aboard the vessels like cattle. Jammed into the lower holds of the vessel, inhumanely.

Ironies of life--these men, after surviving almost three years of imprisonment, always with the hopes of being liberated by our forces, survived only to be killed by the bombs and torpedoes of the liberating forces--not all, but most of them, because of being transported in unmarked vessels.

The heat was unbearable in the crowded holds. No sanitation facilities, just a few buckets. Food generally a thin mixture of rice (called *lugao* by the Filipinos) which was lowered to them in buckets. Water was almost non-existent. Some of the survivors spent over 30 days in these holds and had to face additionally the death dealing weapons of the American forces. Helpless, trapped in the holds of these vessels, they could do nothing but hope. Those men participated in a carnage almost unknown to mankind. Slaughtered. One remarked, "Hell has to be a letdown after this."

The following is an excerpt from a book written by John Tolanda, *The Rising Sun* (New York: Random House,

1970), pp. 679-681.

*...in the afterhold the other 600 men were experiencing the same hell. They had been given a skimpy meal of rice and fish, but no water. Most of them had unthinkingly emptied their canteens during the hot march through the streets. They began fanning the air in unison with mess kits, but it made no difference. The men stripped in the oven like heat. In the darkness they shouted for water but the guards ignored them; their own comrades had come to the Philippines in the same holds, if not as crowded. The prisoners' exertions exhausted the oxygen from the air. One man, suffocating, toppled over silently with remarkable restraint, but others, gasping for breath, thrashed about wildly before collapsing. A dozen, crazed by thirst, went berserk, they slashed at the throats and wrists of companions to suck blood. The panic turned the hold into bedlam. To Major Virgil McCullum, another veteran of Bataan, it was "the most horrible experience imaginable and probably unprecedented in the annals of civilization." As the dim light filtered through the hatch, several score bodies lay lifeless...suffocated or murdered.*

*From topside, the men heard excited shouting. There was the bark of anti aircraft guns, and shards of glass showered through the hatches. Bombs pummeled the ship and machine gun bullets clattered noisily along the decks above. In the afterhold, the prisoners clawed up ladders, terrified lest they be trapped below, but were driven back by guards firing down in their midst. The bombers returned at half hour*

85

*intervals.*

*Those in the forward hold faced another night of horror. There were shouts of "quiet" and "at ease" but as the temperature reached 119 degrees, riots erupted. It was the worst and most brutal period of Colonel Beecher's life. All around him men were going mad. They collided with one another in the dark, slipping and sliding in the feces; the sick were trampled, wild deadly fights erupted. Men dropped to knees like animals to lap up sewage running in the open drains.*

*"Many lost their minds," a Colonel later wrote in his official report, "and crawled about in the absolute darkness with knives attempting to kill people in order to drink their blood or armed with canteens filled with urine and swinging in the dark. The hold was so crowded and everyone so interlocked with each other that the only movement possible was over the heads and bodies of others."*

*Shortly after dawn , the first twenty-five men started up the ladder. The interpreter called for another twenty-five. As they started up the ladder, the interpreter frenziedly waved them back: "many planes, many planes."*

*A bomb crashed into the rear of the Oryoko Maru. The blast hurled shrapnel throughout the aft hold. Superstructure tumbled down the hatchway pinning screaming men. Flames swept through the wreckage. More than 100 of the trapped prisoners were dead; 150 were dying."*

When it was over the total casualties on the Oryoko Maru were 1426 prisoners dead out of 1800 prisoners.

This is only part of the story of what occurred on one "Hell Ship." Here is a short accounting of what happened on another one, the *Arisan Maru*. She left the Philippines with 1803 prisoners aboard, out of which only eight survived. I repeat 8, after a day's bombing.

Following are the statistics for other Japanese vessels transporting prisoners out of the Philippines:

| Vessel | #PoWs Aboard | # Killed | Date |
|---|---|---|---|
| Tatori Maru | 1800 | 11 | 10/08/42 |
| Umeda Maru | 1500 | 15 | 10/07/42 |
| Nagoto Maru | 1700 | 157 | 11/07/42 |
| Taga Maru | 850 | 70 | 09/43 |
| Shinyo Maru | 750 | 668 | 10/04/44 |
| Haro Maru | 1100 | 39 | 10/44 |
| Arisan Maru | 1803 | 1795 | 10/10/44 |
| Unknown Maru | 1100 | 1100 | 10/16/44 |
| Oryoko Maru | 1803 | 1426 | 12/13/44 |

**Total Prisoners Killed on Hell Ships -- 5281**

I was on the *Tatori Maru*, the first ship to leave the Philippines in 1942, for about 30 days. We were attacked by an American submarine in the China Sea firing two torpedoes at us. They only fired two torpedoes and I presume they had no more as we were "sitting ducks" and all alone out there. We somehow all survived the attack, but looking at the statistics of the other "hell ships," it looks like we were on a pleasure cruise boat, relatively speaking, as we only had eleven dead when we finally arrived in Formosa.

I have often wondered what had happened to whatever Intelligence we had in the Philippines; couldn't they have alerted the American forces that American POWs were being transported on unmarked Jap vessels? Obviously not.

American prisoners wave off planes attacking transport ship. Sketch by Col. E. Jacobs

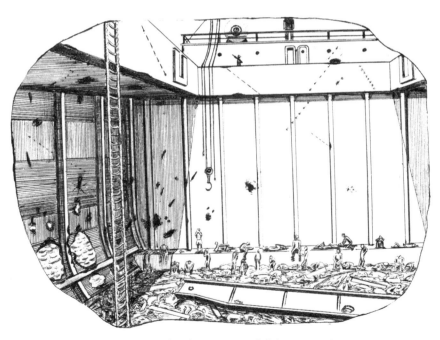

Through the shrapnel gash . . . 300 mangled American prisoners.
Sketch by Col. E. Jacobs

Volumes could be written on Jap brutality. They imprinted another large stain on their image in the "Palawan Massacre." Approximately 300 American POWs were detailed there by the Japs to construct an airfield out in the jungles. When the task was completed, half of the men were transferred to other prison camps and 150 men were left in Palawan to maintain the facility. After an American air raid, the Japs allowed the prisoners to dig air raid shelters in the prison yard. One day the air raid alarm sounded and the Japs allowed the prisoners to go to their shelters. No planes appeared but the men were ordered to stay in their shelters. Suddenly, some Japs appeared with gasoline and lit torches. They threw gasoline into the shelters followed by the lighted torches. Screaming men ran from the shelters, clothing and bodies aflame, to be met by Japanese bayonets and rifle fire. One hundred forty Americans perished that day, 10 escaping up a cliff in the confusion and then swimming some miles across the bay into friendly Filipino hands.

You can appreciate why it is so difficult for some of us to forgive them. Laughing, yes, laughing Japs, burning, bayonetting and shooting helpless men. I bet they scored well with their sun god that day.

Throughout this narrative, I have generally referred to the Japanese as "Japs." In prison camp we usually called them Japs or Nips (from Nipponese). They don't like to be referred to this way. I wonder, if it offends their finer "sensibilities." The bastards; right now I hate them all over again--even the Japanese should hate them.

## 26

One bright morning in December 1944, we became aware of the sound of many aircraft approaching. Looking up into the sky, we saw to our amazement formation after formation of American aircraft approaching. We whistled and cheered, but not for long. In a few moments we were hearing again the old familiar swishing and whistling of falling bombs. We hit the dirt fast as the whistling continued.

As luck would have it, several bombs hit right inside the prison compound. Shades of Bataan and Corregidor all over again. Nineteen of our group were killed and about 40 wounded. The American pilots had no way of knowing that our prison camp was situated right next door to the factory they were bombing. They hit the factory, too.

Jubilation sort of faded as we ministered to our sick, dying and dead. However, it basically was a great uplift and rallying factor to us. Seeing our own planes once again flying overhead and knowing that we must be winning the war. Our fatalities were just the fortunes of war, once again.

Shortly after this, the Japs allowed us to dig foxholes in the prison compound which we used whenever there was an air raid alarm. There were not many and fortunately we were not bombed again.

Another great day was the day the Japs issued us mail from home that had been sent via the Swiss Red Cross. The first mail I received contained over 400 letters from my sister Dale alone. The Japs must have had it for a very long time before they issued it. It was so good and comforting to hear from our loved ones again after so many years. Tears flowed from my eyes as I read my mail. Everyone read everyone else's mail, we just passed our letters around. Many a tear was shed that day. It was so sad for those who received no mail and for the few who received "Dear John" letters.

Some of us also received personal packages from home. Our families were only permitted to send us one package. Those of us who received packages were like little children at a birthday party opening their gifts. Almost everyone shared their package with those who did not receive one. It was a banner day for us, even though we felt like yo-yos on a string of happiness and despair.

Part of food and other supplies dropped by American
Planes into prison camp, the day after liberation.

## 27

One day our prison gates opened to admit a large group of bedraggled prisoners--about 300. Gaunt, sick, pitiful survivors from bombed or torpedoed hell ships--many from the *"Oryoko Maru."* Among the new prisoners were three Catholic priests. We had not seen a chaplain of any denomination in almost three years since leaving the Philippines. One of the priests still had his altar stone and some vestments.

The Japs said that we could hold religious services for one hour on Sundays. The first Mass I attended after all the years was a spiritual experience I will never forget and always treasure. One unusual aspect of the service was, that it was celebrated without the usual bread and wine in the rituals. Obviously, we had none.

With instructions from the priests, we set about making bread wafers and wine. Men who had raisins left from their food packages pooled them. Johnny and I added water to them in accordance with instructions from the priests and placed the mixture in a stolen bucket under the ground in the hen house. We buried it to prevent the Japs from discovering it. At the end of two weeks, we had "sacramental wine," three small medicine bottles full. Men stole flour when they were on detail in the Jap warehouse, stuffing their pockets with it. Someone in camp fashioned a crude set of tongs, the ends of which were shaped to form a circular wafer--only they were at least 1/2 inch thick. One asked, *"Father, should we make a collection basket too, so the ceremony will be truly Catholic?"*

Men of all faiths attended the services which comforted and aided us and, as I have said, provided a tremendous uplift, impacting strongly on us all. We held clandestine services at other times than Sundays through an elaborate surveillance system we developed. While the service was going on in one of the barracks, we had men strategically positioned in the camp compound to give notice of any Jap guards approaching the barracks. We were never discovered, but often had to terminate services quickly.

I should note, that had the Chaplains been of any other faiths, they would have been welcomed with the same enthusiasm and joy.

From the new arrivals we learned, that the Americans were somewhere in the Philippines and fighting their way towards Japan proper. We were heartened by the news...perhaps the end was really in sight...please, not a rumor...dear God, let it be true.

The new arrivals couldn't believe the food we were getting in this camp: cornmeal (and they loved it), kaoliang (barley), watery soup with perhaps a tiny bit of meat in it, and a small bread roll each day. They also loved the soybeans.

We oldtimers in the camp didn't realize it but prison-fare wise we were relatively well fed. Maybe we were spoiled. One of the new arrivals said that it was like eating at the Waldorf--and he was serious.

# 28

Two of the Japs were transferred from our camp at this time. Captain Ishikawa, the "Bull," and that other son of a bitch, Corporal Noda, the "Rat." Brutal beatings practically ceased, although severe punishments for infractions were still meted out and men were still sent to the "guard house" for detention in cells that had no heat at all. This was a serious punishment in the climes we were experiencing--temperatures down to 40-45 degrees below zero.

Once in a while the guards would get mean and tough, particularly after some bombing of Japan or after word of some new American victory. On the whole, the situation was more bearable, even though we still lacked needed medications. If you became seriously ill, your chances were slim. Many prisoners died of diphtheria due to lack of medicines.

I believe most of the Japs knew they were losing the war at this time. I felt the most pressing question before them was how to pursue a path to peace with a face saving solution. Some of the fanatics did not consider surrendering at any price. Unconditional surrender was not an option they could consider because they wanted to preserve the Royal House, Emperor Hirohito, the living God. If the atomic bomb had not been dropped, no one could have predicted when they would have surrendered. Their face saving mania was exacerbated in their relations with foreign cultures. I feel, they actually had an inferiority complex attitude in their contacts with other nationalities. Were these characteristics, however, the driving force that made them such fierce adversaries and after the war led them to become one of the foremost economic powers in the world? And you know, they have won WWIII.

* * * * * * * *

Several years after the war ended, I was employed by a large U.S. corporation and principally involved with new ship construction. In those years, the Japanese were the largest shipbuilding nation in the world and they built among the best of new ships coming off the ways of worldwide ship builders. In conjunction with my work, I made many trips to various shipyards in Japan. I found them extremely intelligent, courteous, and ostensibly friendly. I had to meet with them many times for engineering discussions concerning the equipment we were furnishing for the new ship construction. Inwardly, I was never quite at ease, especially during the many hours I was obliged to spend with them at dinner parties and other social functions, which is the traditional Japanese manner of "doing business." In our discussions, I would inevitably revert to speaking to them in Japanese. They would always remark on my good accentuation and idiomatic use of their language and always asked me where I had learned to speak Japanese. I didn't tell them that I had personal instruction from great teachers who "pounded their language into me. I would comment that I had been a "guest of the Emperor" for 3-1/2 years. All of them would become extremely embarrassed and apologize to me. (The "so solly" routine again.) In fairness to them, they didn't know what was going on in their prison camps, and I am sure that the majority of their population didn't know either. However, I still had a feeling that I could never embrace them; a feeling that I would be untrue to the memory of all those men who had perished as a

94

result of the cruelty inflicted upon them. There was an invisible wall between us, that at the time I didn't feel could ever be torn down. In the ensuing years most, but not all, of the wall has fallen. I shall always remember...and I cannot buy a Japanese car ever!

Author far right, discussing technical Ship Building
details with officials at Kawasaki Shipyard, Japan, 1964.

# 29

The Japs eventually provided us with shower facilities at Mukden. We used them a lot in the summer months but in the winter, no way! The water was cold, cold, cold. Only some kind of nut would attempt a shower in the winter months. Winters were long and summers were short in Manchuria, so the Japs had no problems with their water bills in our camp. Most of us did not shower from October to May. We always had lice or bed bugs of some sort and were not unfriendly to them; after all, they were trying to keep warm too. The barracks were always cold, and as I have mentioned, we received only one bucket of coal per day per barracks. This would generally last from 5-6 hours and it was primarily the body heat generated by men in close confines that kept us from freezing.

We all washed our hands and faces daily and I used to shave twice a week. The majority of men grew beards. Interestingly, I used the same Gillette double edged razor blade for over three years. It was kept sharpened by first running the fingers through the hair to pick up any body oil one may have, then running the fingers around the inside rim of a glass tumbler to transfer any oil that may have been accumulated, and then stropping the razor blade by running it around the inside rim of the glass for a long time.

I don't believe the manufacturers of razor blades would want this information publicized.

\* \* \* \* \* \* \* \*

Christmas time in prison was generally a melancholy time with acute memories of family and home celebrations. We all talked about our own family customs in celebrating Christmas. Most of us wondered if we would ever celebrate another one back home with our families.

For Christmas of 1944, the Japs gave each man a 1/4 pound meat ration. It was a large stocking full of cheer to all of us and personally I thought it was one of the best presents I have ever received at Christmas time. I don't know how prisoners in other Japanese camps fared, but this munificent gesture occurred in our prison camp in Mukden.

The cooks made a thick stew of it with potatoes and carrots, and it was simply delicious--a gourmet's delight. All it needed with it was a bottle of Chateau-Neuf-de-Pape '73 and an after dinner brandy.

Americans must be getting closer, we thought.

The Japs also permitted us to stage a Christmas show and, surprisingly, most of them attended. The men devised numerous skits, men costumed as women with long blond tresses of straw and huge stuffed breasts doing the Can-Can, wearing nothing under their skirts; several men and women comedy routines; and music by the *Mukden Snowballs*. Jack Rogers and I performed on the guitars.

It was nice to enter this world of make believe again, if only for an evening. The Japs topped off the evening by giving each man two cigarettes. The treatment was softening--at least this day.

Speaking about cigarettes. They were our monetary medium and means for bartering in prison. Men would exchange clothing for cigarettes, and what was most heart rending to see was a sick and dying prisoner offering his food ration for cigarettes. I have seen emaciated men stumbling around with their food ration in one hand, bartering it for a cigarette. When a Jap threw away the cigarette he had been smoking, everyone in the vicinity would make a grab for the cigarette butt--including me.

The small butt would be smoked by holding it in a toothpick whittled from a piece of wood.

October, 1944. Cabanatuan Hospital, Ward 7. Sketch by Col. E. Jacobs.

# 30

A new Jap officer arrived in our camp near the end of 1944. His name was Hegecata. He was a graduate of Oxford University and his English was impeccable. He also was a member of an illustrious and wealthy family in Japan. He was compassionate towards us and, I believe, partly responsible for the unusual treatment we received at Christmas. We spoke together many times and he often gave me a packet of cigarettes, which was an unusually munificent gesture, as cigarettes were a rationed item to the Japanese. He confidentially confirmed that he knew Japan could not win the war, primarily because of the industrial might of the U.S. He stated, he doubted that the Jap War Machine in Tokyo would ever accept unconditional surrender, but that there was a strong feeling among Japanese intellectuals that it was only a matter of time until they would have to capitulate, due to the shortages of critical and strategic materials such as steel, coal, iron, and food.

When we were liberated by the Russians, our commanding officer, Major Hankins, arranged to have Hegecata taken prisoner by the American forces (all of the Japanese did not want to be taken prisoners by the Russians).

I obtained Hegecata's sword at the time of surrender and would return it to him were it possible to find him. He was an officer and a Gentleman, but more so, a compassionate and kind person. I wish him well, wherever he may be today.

Besides Hegecata and perhaps Colonel Matsudo, I feel there were some other Japanese persons whom I should acknowledge for their compassion and good will during those times.

Semopo Sugibar, Japanese Consul in Lithuania, helped over 4,000 Jewish people escape from the Nazi's by issuing them Japanese visas, enabling them to travel across the Soviet Union.

A Japanese soldier, name unknown, whom I observed in a kneeling position with helmet off beside the bunk of an American prisoner of war, who was obviously close to death. I watched, as he laid his rifle down and made the sign of the cross and prayed while holding the hand of the dying prisoner. An honorable warrior and compassionate foe after the battle.

Kawashima, one of our interpreters and guards in Mukden. Born in Hawaii, educated for a while in American schools, he honestly tried to help the prisoners as much as his limited position would allow. He was the one to tell me to quickly stand up each time after the "Bull" was beating me. Once in a while he would relay to us the progress of the war, but at that time we did not know whether to believe him or not. He was a good person and I hope he is alive and back in his beloved Hawaii.

A Japanese seaman on the *Tatori Maru* transporting us to Manchuria. He would surreptitiously give the prisoners cans of food during the voyage as well as medicines.

There were others, too, but not many.

\* \* \* \* \* \* \* \*

I recall one day looking up into the sky and my eyes strayed to the top of the brick wall surrounding our compound. Through the coiled barbed wire I saw the top of a tree blooming and with green leaves. My eyes began to smart at its beauty and the sudden realization that I had not seen green grass, trees, or even a bush in almost three years. Apparently, this tree had grown during the time we were there and was now peeking over our wall.

Looking up at the sky, especially at night, reminded me of what Abraham Lincoln once said:

> *I never behold the stars that I do not feel that I am looking in the face of God. I can see how it might be possible for a man to look down upon the earth and be an atheist, but I cannot conceive how he could look up into the heavens and say, there is no God.*

Japanese landing on Corregidor - May 1942                    (National Archives)

*31*

Things you learn--rice, for instance. When we were first captured our diet consisted of nothing but rice. However, many of the older men who had previous histories of stomach ulcers claimed that the rice diet had cured their ulcers and their stomachs never felt better, apart from their hunger. I often heard them say, *"I am hungry, but I never felt better."* The condition "rice belly" that many of us experienced--I don't know if it came from eating rice or from malnutrition. I suspect the latter.

We used to joke about the Lord's Prayer, saying it should be changed to "and give us this day our daily rice."

It is said that time is a healer. I don't know for sure. Time helps arrange your mind so that you can place sorrowful, even ugly events in the back of it and out of the present. Filed away, but never forgotten. When you want to, you can reach back into the recesses of your mind and recall an incident so vividly that you can't wait to push it into the back of your mind again. With time, however, there is less sorrow and pain as you reopen the files.

I previously mentioned rats. We were forced to cohabitate with brown rats and black rats, but for some reason we did not hate them. However, there were some rats we did hate. These were the "white rats" among us, human, and yet completely inhumane. White rats are deceitful, disgusting, harmful and, unfortunately, not easily killed. They are people--humans, of a very low caste. Self centered, selfish and amoral men who committed the most

102

heinous of crimes possible in a prison camp--"Stool Pigeons" for the Japs. Difficult to believe! These men, I should say creatures, for some extra food, cigarettes, or other favors, revealed to the Japanese the activities of their fellow prisoners. Like planned escapes, secret meetings, stealing from the Japs, sabotage committed by some of our men working in the factory, and so on.

We knew who some of these white rats were and, thankfully, there were very few. Those who survived were reported to military authorities after the war was over. In one case, a Sergeant Provoo on Corregidor was in the midst of the Japanese shortly after our capture. He had apparently studied in Japan prior to the war and was fluent in their language and customs. He would appear in Japanese robes and sandals and issue orders to the American prisoners. It was alleged that he was responsible for the execution of one of the American officers on Corregidor and he was tried after the war for his collusion with the enemy. He was sentenced to life imprisonment but was eventually freed due to legal technicalities. I have never heard of any of the other white rats being tried for their treason. I suppose, the evidence was considered hearsay and I believe it was reasoned that even those who might be guilty had a lower threshold of tolerance and endurance for the conditions experienced and that their years of imprisonment were punishment enough. This is my own surmise of this situation.

I wonder, if any of them alive today have any pangs of conscience for the beatings, punishments, and other deprivations other prisoners suffered as a result of their perfidy. Probably not.

I have heard that in several instances justice was meted out to these treacherous characters in some of the POW camps by other prisoners. I suspect this is true.

# 32

Sundays were now days of leisure and we were not required to work. The Japs allowed us to play baseball and we formed a league consisting of teams from each barracks. We played intensely and extremely competitively. The umpires lived a very precarious and dangerous life and we had difficulty recruiting them. At times you would have thought that you were back in Ebbets Field, watching the Dodgers play. It was a great outlet for our pent-up emotions.

We also had classes, some kind of schooling, for any of the men who were interested. We had instructions in electrical engineering, architecture, music, philosophy, auto mechanics, marine trades (which I taught), etc. I attended the philosophy sessions which were lectured by a Captain Pete Lester, a brilliant man. I recall having to explain to him in one of the sessions my concept of "beauty." My reply was that beauty was primarily "in the eye of the beholder," etc. He explained, all I was saying was that I thought the object I beheld was beautiful. Not a good definition because it does not consider any other criteria for beauty. Also, we cannot look at an object and consider that it alone possesses beauty. According to him, beauty inheres partly in the beholder and partly in the beheld; and the concept of beauty is a relationship between the two (Pete, I hope I didn't screw up explaining this!)

I don't think I was Pete's brightest student, but I was among his most interested. I remember (with difficulty) his lecture on beauty in music. He stated that music was a presentative art (glad I remembered that, it sounds good) and is the emotional relationship between music and the hearer, which leads one to say, "*It is beautiful.*"

The classes were successful, primarily because they uplifted our minds and for a short time our spirits, as we dwelt on thoughts which had nothing (and everything) to do with our will to survive our present circumstances.

Another Sunday, and the Japs brought in an exhibition of Japanese art for us to view. I just don't know why. We speculated, probably to impress us with their culture, samples of which we had endured for several years so far. I must confess though, that I was greatly impressed with the beauty expressed in their art. I was perplexed at the same time; enigmatically so--how could such brutal people create such beauty? The "Kakemono's" paintings on silk, delicate strokes in black and whites with perhaps a bold splash of bright cherry red, only one in a spot that can be interpreted as a bird on a cherry tree. You have to imagine the completed form of the bird as the outline is suggestive only, similar to Picasso's paintings.

Calligraphy art. Again the bold, then timid strokes; Chinese or Japanese characters executed beautifully in black ink on white rice paper.

Lt. Hegecata explained the calligraphy to me. The characters are for beauty, reason, and virtue and these are the poetic symbols for jade. The beauty I can see, but the other symbols--no way. He explained, and I tried to understand: jade is obviously a beautiful stone, hence beauty. Like reason, jade cannot be destroyed, hence reason. Like virtue, jade cannot be soiled, hence virtue.

I'm still not sure I understand it. However, as old Pete would have said,

> *Beauty is in the eye of the beholder as well as in the perception and it is pleasing to the senses.*

*Some beauty is sensed through the feelings and cannot be seen, such as the beauty in music which can transcend you out of reality to lofty heights of feelings and give you an inner glow.*

I have finally thought of a good definition of beauty that I should have used in my classes at Mukden: "A sirloin strip steak, medium rare, mounds of mashed potatoes, smothered in gravy, a Caesar salad, and a bottle of Burgundy." I am sure Pete would have given me 100% for this definition or another one, "the beauty of not being in prison camp...."

And one final thought on my finding the artwork of the Japanese beautiful--was it beautiful because it actually possessed beauty, as Pete said it must, or was it beautiful because my soul was starved for beauty, I wonder....

# 33

Vera Britton was an English author of WWI vintage who suffered deeply in that war. Her husband, brother, and other relatives were all killed somewhere in France. She wrote about the war and was unrelentlessly bitter; not towards the Germans, but towards the war itself. To me, her words eloquently express the sorrow, despair, the horror and often times the futility of war.

She wrote:

*The dugouts have nearly all blown in, the wire entanglements are a wreck, and in among the chaos of splintered timber and twisted iron and shapeless earth, are the fleshless blackened bones of simple men, who poured out their red, sweet wine of youth unknowing for nothing more tangible than honor of their country's glory or another's lust for power.*

*Let him who thinks war is a golden, glorious thing; who loves to roll forth stirring words of exhortation, praise, valor, and love of country; with as thoughtless and fervid a faith as inspired the priests of Baal to call on their own slumbering deity; let him but look at a little pile of sodden, gray rags that cover half a skull and a shin-bone that might have been its ribs; or at this skeleton lying on its side, resting, half crouching as it fell...perfect, but that it is headless, with the tattered clothing still draped around it...look at him and realize how grand and glorious a thing it is to have distilled all youth, joy, and life into a fetid heap of putrescence.*

*Who is there who has seen and known, who can say that even victory is worth the death of one of these?*

A poignant and powerful piece against war. I empathize with her because of her loss and understand her bitterness, too. I have also seen most of what she writes about as have most men in wars. I hate war too, and so does anyone else who has been in one. However, there are certain values we must all consider when war threatens. Pride of country, defense of country, righteousness of our cause, and love of country. These were the considerations that caused millions of Americans and other nationalities to respond and volunteer to serve their country. After the sneak attack on Pearl Harbor and the carnage Hitler was inflicting on Europe, there was no other choice but to fight.

Vera Britton's writings reflect the price all nations pay in war. However, we must never forget that if you want to enjoy the benefits offered by your country, you must share in the responsibilities.

This was the way I felt when I volunteered in 1941. I was sent to the Philippines and didn't enjoy the war one bit but someone had to be there doing the specific assignment I had. If not I, someone else would have had to be there in my place. I could not selfishly wish those years on someone else. I was there and did my best under the circumstances.

* * * * * * * *

I am reminded that there are two instances when a

108

man feels like a man--when he is fighting in a war or when he is making love.

I prefer the latter situation.

The U.S. Army Mine Planter "Col. George F. Harrison" at dockside, Corregidor, Philippines, prior to the commencement of hostilities. Japanese dive bombers secure direct hits on her in late April 1942, killing four of the crew. She was later salvaged by the Japanese and eventually sunk by American bombers shortly before war's end.

## 34

When I discussed the absence of women in our prison life, I think I made us sound like eunuchs. Far from that. I am sure that those men who were married often had thoughts about resuming the delights of the connubial pillow with their wives and those of us who were not married often thought about our romantic interludes when we were feeling better. The Japs called it "pillowing," roughly translated, "getting a girl in the sack."

Those of us who were single were luckier in this regard. We did not have wives and children to worry about. Most of us thought, too, that the girlfriends we left behind were probably married by now, as evidenced by the many "Dear John" letters received in the first mail from home.

I must confess, though, that I did have one woman I thought a lot about in prison camp; most of the time, in fact. She was my first love and I loved her forever. She was a pretty woman, somewhat older than I, perhaps slightly plump, and she even had a few wisps of gray hair the last time I saw her standing in the sun. She always had a smile on her face; was warm, affectionate, and loving. She was smart as a whip and a fabulous dancer--she was my mother.

Wherever you are now, Mom, I understand the pain and anguish you suffered and endured throughout the war years. I understand because I, too, have been a parent now for many years--just like you and Dad. Your three sons, all fighting in the war; your youngest, Buddy, a combat engineer, fighting with Patton's Army all through Germany;

Raymond, your second youngest, on a mine layer, somewhere on the seas; and I, your oldest, almost two years of missing-in-action status until you learned I was a prisoner of war somewhere in Manchuria. Like all families under similar circumstances, you were war casualties, too.

I heard you lost your "cool" one day during the war when you went to the butcher shop and asked for some meat. I heard, the butcher shouted, *"Lady, don't you know there is a war going on?"*, and you replied, softly at first, *"Do I know there is a war going on?"* and with your voice rising to hysterical heights you continued, *"one of my sons is a Japanese prisoner of war, another is in Germany with Patton, and a third is on the high seas planting mines, and you ask me if I know there is a war going on?"*

I heard there was a hush in the store, the loudest one coming from the butcher. He went to the back of the store, gave you some meat and apologized. I bet he never asked anyone else if they knew there was a war going on.

Mom, the only women I ever missed in prison camp were you and my two sisters. And did I miss your cooking! Your omelettes, roasts, and Yorkshire pudding, those holiday special dishes. You were the best cook in the world and I had better stop mentioning all those great dishes you made as I will probably get indigestion from just thinking about them. I guess the secret ingredient in your cooking was love.

And Mom, I want you to know that you married a great guy, Pop. You had two lovely daughters, Dahlia and Elda, my sisters, who suffered and endured with three brothers in the war.

I always remember what Pop said about being alone: Alone you come into the world; alone you leave it; and in your darkest hour you are alone. You must learn to walk alone. How right he was.

I remember, too, that Pop hardly ever took a drink, but when I finally came home he got drunk at the corner

111

bar with me.  Didn't cost much to get him drunk either.
Two drinks!

Author boarding
U.S.N. Hospital Ship
in Dairen, Manchuria
on first leg of
homeward journey.
Sept 1945.

Author
recouperating
at Brooks General
Hospital. July 1946.

# 35

It was early 1945 in prison camp. As usual, it was extremely cold. Conditions had improved and strong longings for the war to end persisted. Our food had also improved with the addition of a little meat, and a few medicines were trickling in. The medicines were about three years late for most of the men who had not survived but were welcome for those needing it at this time, as we still had many men in the hospital. The Japs, too, were relatively quieter and while punishments were still meted out, they were not as severe as previously and, to my knowledge, there were no more savage beatings.

Time passed somehow--though each day was a repetition of the last. You learned to live each day for itself, not daring to think about tomorrow. It was upsetting and depressing if you did.

We often passed time by telling stories of our pasts. The same stories were repeated by the same men over and over and strangely, everyone was still interested in hearing them. I was often called upon to relate an "adventure" I had experienced a few years prior to the war. Everyone thought it was hilariously funny, except I, because for me it had been a true experience.

I was sitting in a cafe somewhere in Bucharest, Romania, along with a male friend. The year was 1940 and we were sipping our drinks and listening to music. Two ravishingly beautiful women were sitting a few tables away and sending eye messages to us. Being only human, we soon joined them at their table. One was a gorgeous red head with green eyes, and the other was a blue eyed brunette, also beautiful. After an evening of drinking, dancing, touching and kissing (and could that red head kiss!), we made arrangements to adjourn to a nearby hotel.

We sat on the bed just kissing and kissing when I decided it was time to undress and proceeded to do so. My red head was apparently shy and insisted on turning off the lights before she undressed. I lay in bed, eagerly awaiting the anticipated delights. She crawled into the bed and I reached for her, touching her, when to my horror, yes horror, I discovered I was holding genitals larger than my own. The sons of bitches were gays. I was overcome with nausea over having kissed "him" all evening and I still feel the same way today. I threw him out of the room and in the hallway found my friend beating up his "girlfriend." I have been afraid to pick up a girl ever since.

My fellow prisoners never tired of hearing this story and I don't know how many times I had to repeat it to their howls of delight and taunts.

* * * * * * * *

Death still hovered lightly over us, sort of omnipresent. Most of us believed that we would not live to see the end of the war. If the American forces were approaching, the Japs would move us to prevent our liberation, as they had done to the American prisoners of war in the Philippines. It was an agony of uncertainty at times.

One thing you don't need in a prison camp is a clock. Time stood still. Time meant nothing except another day, week, or year of the same apathetic routine. Each new day was the same, a repetition of the past day. You awoke in the morning and found yourself awake in the same nightmare--never knowing what was going to happen. It becomes burdensome after a long time.

114

You have a cup of "coffee" made from roasting the barley, as I have previously explained. However, when you forgot what real coffee tasted like it really wasn't too bad. After coffee, you wash, that is, if the water isn't too cold. Then line up for *"tenko"*, roll call for the Japs' check of prisoners; then attend to the duties or work detail you are assigned to, and at the end of the day you just sit around and talk--and there is never anything new to talk about-- and then to sleep. During all this time, if you haven't run into an unhappy Jap, you have had a good day.

Work, talk, sleep, dream--that's all there is, except try to be prepared for death whenever it may come because it is hanging around all the time. You are always in the valley of the shadow of death.

I was often reminded of the story of the woman abandoned in the desert with her young child. She struggled for days and days through the hot burning sand with the scorching sun beating down from above. She finally reached the campsite of some nomads who aided her. While recovering from the ordeal she prayed to the Lord. *"Lord, Lord,"* she said, *"in my greatest hour of need, I prayed and prayed to you to help me and my child, but I saw only one set of footprints in the sand when I looked back; why did you forsake me in the hour of my need?"* And she heard the Lord reply, *"My dear child, the reason you saw only one set of footprints in the sand was that they were mine. I was carrying you."*

* * * * * * * *

Our cemetery at this time was, fortunately, not receiving many new occupants. Out of the original group there were approximately 1000 men alive. Our annual spring burials were practically over (spring burials, meaning the mass burials of all those men who had died during the winter months, the bodies waiting for the spring thaw so

115

graves could be dug), and we had only a few dead to bury this year. The arrival of Spring was always announced by the terrible stench of the decaying bodies in the warehouse where they were stored during the winter months. On the small crosses we were permitted to erect over each grave, we would engrave the name, rank, serial number, and date of death of the deceased. We were so hardened that rarely a tear was shed anymore. We had lived with death so long that it was almost a constant companion and not a stranger. Someone always said a prayer, a few headshakes, and a sad journey back to prison.

In life, most of us don't know how or when we are going to die, but in a Jap prison camp, you could make some pretty good guesses. I suppose, we were miserably hardened to the sad emotions generally associated with death. Even remembering what Seneca said, didn't help much: "The day which thou fearest so much and which thou callest thy last, is the birthday of an eternity." I liked what some French soldier wrote during WWI:

*On Worrying*
*When you are a soldier, you are one of two things;*
*Either at the front or behind the lines.*
*If you are behind the lines, you need not worry.*
*If you are at the front, you are one of two things;*
*You are either in a zone of danger or a zone that is not*
*dangerous.*
*If you are in a zone that is not dangerous, you need not*
*worry.*
*If you are in a zone that is dangerous, you are one of*
*two things;*
*You will be either wounded or not wounded.*
*If you are not wounded, you need not worry.*
*If you are wounded, you are one of two things;*
*Either slightly wounded, or seriously wounded.*
*If you are slightly wounded, you need not worry.*

*If you are seriously wounded, one of two things is certain;*
*Either you get well or you die.*
*If you get well, you need not worry.*
*If you die, you cannot worry.*
*So there is no need to worry about anything at all.*

Author's mother, Angela and father, Conrad.

## 36

It is now April 1945 and we have been prisoners a long, long time. It is hard for me to realize that we survivors have endured so long. It feels like an eternity since we were captured. Most of us were not in too bad a condition, due to the small increase in food, mainly a little meat or fish added to our diet and the few medicines that were now available for the very sick. I suppose, we the survivors were the stronger ones, and I should also say, so far the "luckier" ones. Some men were actually released from the camp hospital. Someone said that those in the hospital were having their prayers answered to get them out of prison. I don't know if anyone ever really thought that, but there was no denying that death was a kind release for many. However, most of us thought we would never get out alive.

In July 1945, we again heard the rumor that the Japs were making rice balls, strongly indicating that another move of the prisoners was coming. We deduced that the war must be going badly for them and many of us were seriously considering escaping if we learned they were actually going to move us. Viewed against the probability of more "death marches," more "shell ships," and more "box-car rides," most of us felt that our chances for survival would be no less if we escaped. Another favorable factor at this time was that the weather was warm and we would not have to contend with the bitterly cold weather of the winter months. We also agreed that the Manchurians would be receptive to us, especially if the war was going against the Japs. However, as events unfolded, they did not move us--perhaps they realized it was almost impossible to transport us across the seas to Japan due to the presence of the American naval vessels in the area. Or, perhaps, someone up there was watching out for us and said "enough."

In early August 1945, we heard rumors that a secret type of bomb had been dropped on Japan. Prisoners working in the factory heard that news from some Manchurians. However, to most of us it was just another rumor we were fearful of accepting. The letdowns experienced after years of rumors that all proved to be untrue were difficult to cope with. Most of us, as I said, were dubious about the truth of the rumor. However, a heartening factor was that we were hearing the air raid sirens more often. Some days later, we again heard that another secret bomb was dropped on Japan. We also learned from men working at the factory that Russia was going to invade Manchuria. In view of all these happenings, I was beginning to hope that there was some truth in the rumors.

The Jap guards were strangely quiet and actually sort of friendly. On August 16, 1945 we heard again strong rumors that the Japs had surrendered. Most of us were hopeful and almost believing until we heard another crazy rumor that the Japs were going to move us further north to prevent our release to American forces. I say again that it was like being on a yo-yo of hope and despair; from the heights of hope to the plunging depths of despair. It was a rough time.

On this same day, we heard the droning of an aircraft flying low over the vicinity of the prison camp. It circled around and suddenly we saw six parachutists floating from the sky. They landed outside the prison camp. We later learned that they were taken into custody by the Japanese and brought to the Japanese quarters in the prison camp where they were secluded. We all concluded that the plane

119

must have been Japanese since we were not familiar with the silhouettes of the newer American aircraft. At this time, we also did not know that this was a team of O.S.S. men and a branch of the U.S. military none of us knew about. They also wore American uniforms that were strange to us. Someone reported that they still had their side arms while they were with the Japs; something big was happening!

The next day we learned that the senior officers in our camp had been taken over to the Japanese commanding officer and told that an armistice had been declared but that the Russians and Japanese were still fighting and that we could not leave the prison compound. The war was over, but we still were confined--which didn't bother most of us. Confined, but free.

On August 17, 1945, we were startled to see some Russian tanks and vehicles enter the compound. Russians rounded up all the Japs in the camp and the Russian commander announced Mukden had been secured and "from this hour, all prisoners are free." Chills ran up and down my spine and I believe I was actually shaking. The moment we had waited for all these years had actually arrived. An Australian shouted, *"absofuckinglutely free!"* Everyone broke out in cheers and shouts of joy. I never thought I would be cheering the Russians, let alone loving them.

One thing that puzzled me was that the Japs in our prison camp must have known the war was over on August 15th. Why didn't they inform us at that time?

The Japanese were marched to one side of the compound where they formally surrendered to us. General Parker was the senior officer in our camp at this time. A nice gesture was extended by the command when they allowed Major Hankins to accept Colonel Matsuda's sword. Major Hankins had been our senior officer for almost three years until the arrival of the higher ranks in our prison camp, some short time previously.

120

Selected American prisoners under the command of Lt. Jake Levie marched the **Jap prisoners** (what a great delight to write those words) to the Guard House. The captors became the captured and not a goddamned one of them attempted hara-kiri in accordance with their Bushido and Samurai codes. A lot of men were disappointed. *"Japanese soldier never be prisoner; he will be first kill himself,"* from one of the countless addresses by the Japanese to us during our imprisonment. What are you going to say to your Sun God now, and how are you ever going to explain the severe "loss of face" you exhibited today? When we are captured, we are not expected to commit hara-kiri; we are expected to try to live; escape when possible; and attempt to rejoin our forces so we can continue fighting. However, when I look back over the years of captivity, perhaps a lot of us would have been better off if we had committed hara-kiri.

After the Japs were marched off and our initial shouts of joy and disbelief had quieted, many of us burst into tears. We were given the gift of life again and the great gift of freedom which most people can't appreciate unless it is taken from them. We would see our loved ones again; we made it! It was just too much to handle emotionally. Tears were the only possible way of release for years of pent up emotions. Tears of joy, and of sorrow too. Joy for ourselves, and sorrow for those who had died among us and were not here to share in this day. It was also confusing, bewildering, and still difficult to accept--a dream come true.

The dam, holding back so many unbearable and so many loving memories burst. Tensions were abruptly ending and the nightmare was over for the present though it will be forever tattooed in our minds. Life subject to the capricious whim of the captor was over too. No more bowing or jumping to attention for any Jap; no more punishments or beatings; and no more cornmeal (I do not eat it to this day)!

121

August 17th, however, will always be one of the happiest days of my life. Incidentally, August 17th is also the birthday of my mother. "Happy birthday, Mom--and I have a very special present for you on this birthday--ME!"

The euphoria surrounding our release led us to hug one another; congratulate one another; sing songs like "California, Here I Come"; merriment with tears in our eyes. Dan and I just hugged each other and couldn't say a word.

We all talked about the first things we were going to do; no, not women; no, not booze; just eat food like hamburgers, milkshakes, steak, hot dogs, and drink gallons of milk.

I wandered outside of the prison compound and saw green grass, trees, and green bushes with some flowers. I was overwhelmed by all the beauty in nature that I had been deprived of and never really appreciated before. I saw some little Manchurian children huddled around their mothers and they all smiled and waved at me. I hadn't seen a child or women in 3 1/2 years and returned their salutation with moist eyes. I still couldn't believe I was free, free, free. It was so delicious.

We were told we could go into town. I couldn't find Dan so I went in with two other men. On the way in, a young Manchurian man stopped us and invited us to his home for dinner. They apparently were an affluent family judging by the food they served us. Dish after dish of the tastiest food I had ever had. They recounted their hardships under Japanese rule and, obviously, had a deep hatred for them ever since they were conquered. They, too, were jubilant at being liberated from the Japs.

We continued on into Mukden proper. On the way we commandeered a horse and a buggy from some man. We found out where the local brewery was located and proceeded there, loading up the buggy with all the beer it could hold. Some other ex-POWs (even now, its great to write that "ex") came along and said, the buggy was too

122

small so they went down the road to the firehouse and took one of the fire engines, loading it up with beer. With screaming sirens they returned to the prison camp. A lot of beer was consumed that day; however, it only took about two beers to get you drunk.

The next day we heard the drone of American planes overhead. They approached the prison camp and we looked on in amazement as the sky filled up with falling parachutes. They were dropping canisters of food, medicines, clothing, candy, cigarettes; everything except girls. Everyone rushed out to retrieve the containers. I recall the first thing I ate was a can of corned beef and several chocolate bars--and I was sick after that but didn't mind a bit.

The doctors cautioned about eating too much of the food at one time as our bodies could not assimilate the rich foods in this radical new diet dropped upon us from the heavens. To you men who fought in the war while we were captured, I understand that you hated "C" rations. The first can of "C" rations I tasted was sublime; a gastronomical delight to all of us. My youngest brother, Buddy, who fought as a combat engineer in Europe, still complains about the "K" rations he had to eat during the war. I guess you had to be a POW to appreciate it.

We outfitted ourselves in the new clothing dropped. Most of the men shaved off their beards and we started to look like humans again. Sometimes we had trouble recognizing each other.

The pent up emotions harbored throughout all the prison years were slowly disappearing. I think for the first time many of us realized how close we were to each other and how much we really cared about each other. One of our nurses from Bataan and Corregidor eloquently expressed this feeling when she said, "We are a family."

She is right, we are a loving, close knit, caring family of survivors.

The American planes continued to fly over and

dropping supplies. Our wonderful country had not forgotten us as many had originally thought. They showered us with such wonderful things over the days that followed that it can only be described as "manna" falling from the heavens.

Author with wife, Peggy. 1984.

*(I met Peggy at a resort in the Poconos in early 1947. Two weeks later I married her! I often used to tell an old anecdote concerning our romance--much to her chagrin.*

*When I met her, she told me that her family was in the Iron and Steel business, so I immediately married her with visions of wealth in my mind. After we were married, I learned that her family was in the Iron & Steal business: her mother used to iron and her father to steal!.*

*Peggy and I were married for 38 years, until her death in 1984.)*

## 37

Surprisingly, there was not much evident vindictive-
ness on the part of the ex POWs towards the Japs who were
now our prisoners--or perhaps I should say "detainees"--
locked up in the guard house and guarded by Americans.
They were given the same food that we received, medical
care, and cigarettes. There were one or two instances after
we were first liberated when some of our men "talked" to a
few individual Japs, who all needed dental work afterwards.
None of them were seriously injured. If the "Bull" or the
"Rat" Noda had been there, I shudder to think what might
have happened. I feel that the euphoria of newly found
freedom eliminated any thoughts of personal retribution.

I visited Lt. Hegecata several times, bringing him
cigarettes and returning his kindness to me. I also gave
Colonel Matsuda some cigarettes. I found it somewhat
awkward to have all of them stand up to "attention" and
bow when I entered their prison quarters.

It was at this time that I thanked Hegecata for his
kindness to me. He said that they all feared becoming
prisoners of the Russians and preferred American custody
of them. I promised to try to help and spoke to Major
Hankins about it. He arranged for Hegecata to be turned
over to American custody. Colonel Matsuda and Lieutenant
Murata were eventually turned over to American control for
their appearances before the War Crimes Tribunal. Colonel
Matsuda was hanged as well as the Jap doctor, Lt. Murata.
I never saw or heard from Hegecata again and sincerely

hope that he made it home to his family and loved ones. I still feel Colonel Matsuda's sentence was harsh; but of course, I had no access to the formal charges against him, so I am not in a position to evaluate his sentence. I felt he was an Army regular who followed the directives issued from Tokyo and was in no position to disagree. He just followed orders as most of us would have done under similar circumstances. In general, I found him personally to be a kind, considerate person.

He was no doubt found guilty of issuing the orders for the execution of the three men who escaped from our prison camp. They claimed that the men were not executed for escaping but for the murder of some Jap or Manchurian after they escaped. I suppose, as the Commandant of the prison camp he was indirectly responsible for the conduct and cruel treatment meted out to the prisoners by the "Bull" and the "Rat," Noda. I do not believe Colonel Matsuda knew all of what was going on by the "Bull," Noda, or the Camp Doctor, and I suppose therein lies his guilt.

Following is one of his last addresses to us:

*In the Russo-Japanese War of the 37th year of Meiji (1904-1905), the Japanese Emperor took up arms in the expanses of Manchuria, greatly inferior to the Russian forces, numerically. Tzarist Russia was known to have the greatest military machine of the times and were feared by all the nations ever since Napoleon's disastrous campaign against her. Our colors were fruited with victory after victory, and the formidable army which had been built up with intent to overrun the Orient and with which Russia had expressed intent and every ambition was crumpled up like paper and the cornerstone for peace in the Orient laid.*

*The final pushover was enacted in the*

126

*Battle of Mukden in which the Japanese Force, numerically inferior, attacked the Russian army here in Mukden, Manchuria, and on March the tenth, that is, this day, this month, in the 38th year of Meiji, completely surrounded and annihilated the cream of the Tzar's troops. This day has been set aside as our Army Day. This locality abounds in battlefields of that day and there is something spirit feeling that pervades in the air here.*

*The Japanese people as a race are not pugnacious, but when they take up the sword of righteousness for the Emperor, death to them is as light as a feather and means a return to their fathers. They revere the Just and the Right and are full of compassion for the weak. This is one phase of Bushido. This is what I wish conveyed to you on Army Day.*

*Col. M. Matsuda*
*Commandant, Mukden POW Camp, March 10, 1945.*

Well, Colonel, I believe you sincerely meant your remarks, but what happened to the rest of your gang?

# 38

We were still living in the prison camp, though now a life of relative luxury: all we wanted to eat, well clothed, medical treatment, cigarettes, and all the beer we wanted, too. When our supply ran low, someone would take the fire truck back to the brewery and reload. However, we were all itching to go home. There was a problem, though. The railroad lines were apparently seriously damaged in the bombings and I assume there were no suitable air fields near Mukden to evacuate us by air. We were forced to remain in Mukden about a month longer until the rails were serviceable again. Eventually we were informed that we were to be transported by rail to a seaport in Dairen, Manchuria, then by hospital ship to Okinawa, and finally by air to Manila. We were jubilant as we packed our meager belongings, had a last look at our "home" for almost three years, and boarded the train for Dairen. We arrived that evening at the dockside where the hospital ship was docked.

The sight of the U.S. Hospital Ship *Relief* was a deep emotional experience for all of us. This huge white vessel, blazing in lights, flying the stars and stripes, with blue and white clad sailors greeting us, with nurses, visions in white calling out to us; this was just too much to bear. It was the first time we had seen the American flag in 3 1/2 years. Pent up emotions again poured out in tear filled eyes. It was all so overwhelming that I just couldn't cope with it.

We climbed aboard, gaunt and emaciated men; those unable to walk were carried aboard and the nurses greeted us. Everyone of them was crying. Christ, you would have thought we were celebrities. We were all assigned to beds in the various wards and almost immediately fed. Meat, mashed potatoes, gravy, peas, ice cream, and milk. I thought I had died and gone to heaven.

The greatest surprise were the women nurses. They all looked like movie stars to us, ravishingly beautiful. I said to one of them, *"may I just hold your hand?"* and she replied by grabbing me and hugging me, crying softly as she embraced me. Tears again filled my eyes. Hell, I said to myself, if you keep this up you are going to become dehydrated. There wasn't a dry-eyed nurse in the crowd as they welcomed us. Some of the sailors appeared misty-eyed too. I guess, we were a sorry looking lot.

It is an emotionally packed time when you suddenly find yourself among women after having been away from them for years. She is a wonderful creature, and just wondrous to men who have been deprived of her presence and companionship for such a long time. As the song goes, *"It's been a long, long time."*

I shall always treasure the warmth and compassion showered upon us by these nurses. Their kindness towards us glowed even in the darkness and their pampering was spoiling us...it was just great.

The Chief Nurse on the hospital ship was Ann Bertnititus, who had escaped from Corregidor by submarine some 36 hours prior to the capitulation. It was a memorable day for her too, greeting many of her old comrades in arms.

The second night on board, the nurse on ward invited me and my friend, Jim McEntee, up to the nurses quarters to dance. The nurse, Betty Rivers, from Schenectady, N.Y., was a truly beautiful woman. Blue-eyed, blue-black hair, alabaster white skin, and a warm smile the shone from her eyes. A few other prisoners of war (I should remember to write ex-POWs) were also invited by some of the other

129

nurses. They played music on a recording machine and we danced. I didn't think I could contain the rapture I experienced. The soft music, holding a woman in my arms again after so many years, thoughts of home, being free again, no more thoughts of survival...I was just running away. How could one person have so much luck. My cup truly "runneth over."

(I met Betty again some months after the war was over. She came to New York City and we went out on the town. Dinner at Nino's, a plush dinner lounge on the upper east side, and then on to various night spots until daybreak. We saw each other numerous times after that as I was a patient in a military hospital located near her home. I was hopelessly in love with her and why we never married, I don't know to this day. I imagine it was due to my insecurity and emotional instability at that time. I hope you are having a great life, Betty, wherever you may be.)

The hospital ship finally arrived in Okinawa but no sooner did we get there when a typhoon struck. The vessel put out to sea again to weather the storm that day and night. It was a nasty one with tremendous damage to Okinawa and to many of the vessels in the vicinity. Many of the smaller ones were wrecked or sunk.

Another reminder that there are other hazards and dangers in life, besides those encountered in a prison camp.

# 39

We spent several days in Okinawa after we debarked, with sad farewells to all those wonderful people on the hospital ship. We headed for the officers' club, where we met a Lt. Bob Peoples, who took three of us on a jeep tour of the island. (Bob Peoples was the well known athlete of Olympic fame.) The marines were still flushing Japs out of the numerous caves on the island with flame throwers. The flame thrower was a weapon none of us had ever seen or heard about; it was awesome. I would have enjoyed lighting the cigarettes of a few Japs I knew with it.

We went back to the officers' club for some drinks and really got "bombed." No one at the club would let us pay for a single drink even though I had $50 which I had borrowed from the chief engineer of the hospital ship, who, like myself, was a graduate of the New York State Maritime College. We spent three days on Okinawa, during which we were attended by the medical staff, wined and dined as VIPs. Another great interlude on our journey home.

On the morning of the third day we were loaded aboard B-24s for the trip to Manila, where we were to be bivouacked, pending our transportation to the States. The air trip turned out to be real hairy. We lost one of the engines and the pilot reassured us it was nothing to worry about. Nothing to worry about--after spending three and one half year in prison camps, we were going to crash on our way home! We limped safely into Manila and felt the same way we did when we were liberated by the Russians.

I was more angry than scared over the incident.

In Manila we were billeted in a special area set aside for us. We were issued new uniforms, shoes, underwear, socks, travel cases, and many other things that I can't remember at this time. A special kitchen was set up for us, open 24 hours daily. You could almost order anything at any time of day or night and as many times as we liked: (steak, medium rare, please), hamburgers, french fries, ice cream, milk, milkshakes, apple pie, and almost anything else our hearts desired.

We also were permitted to draw money against our accrued back pay, which was in the many thousands of dollars for most of us. Almost every day in Manila would see Dan and myself at the finance window drawing more money. It meant nothing to us. We had seen the days when no amount of money could buy you a drink of water or a piece of bread, when you were thirsting or starving to death. I guess, we sort of went berserk in an orgy of spending money. Sort of an act of defiance. Taxis to town every day, drinking, night clubs, girls...just fun and frolic in an attempt to wipe out the past few years of our lives. I should say, a vain attempt.

We met two lovely American girls, WACs. Imagine our surprise to find women in the Armed Forces. From what I saw of them, we should have done it a long time ago and not limited their service to the nurse corps, We wined and dined these two girls, Lillian Hughes and Mary Chaffin, as only two ex-POWs could in a mad whirlwind, merry-go-round manner. It wasn't only fun, it was wonderful. I have often wondered if they knew how much they were helping to rehabilitate us. I'll never forget you girls.

What I remember most from those early days in Manila was waking up each morning to the sound of music. The P.A. system would play songs like *"It's been a long, long time"; "I walk alone"; I'll be home for Christmas"; "Evaline";* and so many other songs we were unfamiliar with. The music was comforting and a constant reminder that we were free, free again. We were "home" though in actuality we were thousands of miles from the old homesteads.

I feel we were all emotionally unstable and I don't see how we could have been otherwise. Following are some excerpts from my first letter home which I think is revealing in this regard:

> *. . . I am sort of frightened at the thought of meeting you all again. We are all so emotional. I have made this first meeting with you so many times through the past four years, through musings and vagaries. Now, that it is almost here, I just can't believe it. Believe me when I say that I never really thought I would ever see any of you again here in this life. I trained myself for it and was reconciled to my fate. Alone you come into this world; alone you stand in your moments of greatest trial; and alone you leave this world. A hard philosophy but true. I have been face to face with death so many, many times that I do not stand in awe of it anymore. It's like learning to get along with some person you don't like and can't get away from. Death is a transcendental matter. As one philosopher said, "Life is a dream between two deaths, as death is a dream between two lives."*
>
> *Well, suppose I should digress from such depressing thoughts. Enclosed is a picture of me. Look pretty good, don't I? However, in February 1943, some months after we arrived in Manchuria, I reached my lowest ebb. Was very seriously ill for several months. Malaria, dysentery, pellagra, scurvy, beriberi, and hepatitis. I could only force down a little corn meal mush for food and I was pathetically thin. I think I*

weighed 90-100 lbs. My close friend Dr. Elmer Shabart finally got me back on my feet. He got one of the Japs to bring in some medicine from town called "Duma," which was awful tasting but cured my hepatitis and I became mobile again.

Can't possibly describe how I feel to be free again; however, I might describe it as being dazed and mentally upset. Damaged goods. Living with death so long; the constant strains of survival were hard to cope with for 3 1/2 years. However, it was the uncertainty that took the greatest toll. Believe me, it is great to be rid of our little yellow captors.

There is so much to tell you that I become bewildered at times. Please do not try to make any sort of hero out of me. The thought of it is nauseating to me. I am just a lucky survivor. For some reason I have been more fortunate than those who are not coming home, those who are buried back there--some in graves holding 40-50 bodies. I do not want any glory that they cannot share in. After the battles they still served by enduring starvation, thirst, cruelty, beatings, beheadings, diseases, and almost every other horror related to the Japanese prisoner of war treatment. "Oh God, that bread should be so dear, and flesh and blood so cheap."

I have many close friends here. We are a bizarre group. How are we ever going to be acclimated again to the old way of life. I don't know and it does not really matter--except for the frightened feelings of returning home again. I'm rational enough to know that this feeling is crazy. I always wrote that we would meet again *under the magnolia tree in our garden one day. I can tell you now that I never expected to be there. If we ever were to meet again under a tree, I thought it would be as the Chinese say, a tree in "the valley of many colored grass, by the river of silence."*

*Please do not be alarmed by these vagaries of mine. If I seem inarticulate, it is because I am bewildered. I am very happy deep down at the actual thoughts of our reunion. How I missed and yearned for each of you all the time and it gave me great solace to think about you.*

*In my moments of weakness, I felt like the man who said, "Be good to me, oh God, my boat is so small and the sea so wide...."*

Rereading these old letters reminds me of how all families must have suffered in the war. They, too, bear the scars of wounds that, for some, will never heal.

## 40

Manila, October 1945. We were informed that we would be returned to the U.S. and could choose either air or sea travel. The majority of the ex-prisoners chose sea travel. We embarked on the *S.S. Marine Shark* and had a long and pleasant journey home. By this time most of us had become satiated with food and were starting to act like normal people around it.

It was an emotionally uplifting experience to pass under the Golden Gate Bridge again. More than four years-- at least for most of us. To me it was an awesome sight. Everyone cheered; we were really home now. Some of the families of the men were there to meet them. Screams of joy from tear streaked faces, hugging embraces where no one would let go of the other, men holding their children once again--what a turmoil of joy. The press and newsreels were there too, recording the event. There was a certain sadness in the air, thinking of all those men who too had dreamed of passing under the bridge again one day--but never would.

We were sent to Letterman General Hospital in San Francisco. Everyone on the staff was so good to us. We received the most solicitous care from the medical staff imaginable. They just couldn't do enough for us. We were permitted to leave the hospital whenever we desired to go to town. We were medicated, ate at the finest restaurants, visited the best "watering holes" like Top of the Mark and Joe DiMaggio's Restaurant; and walked on the famous pier eating fresh seafood. Visiting the Top of the Mark Lounge brought back fond memories of the last time I was there over four years ago prior to my departure to the Philippines. Who could have prophesied the next four years for those of us who were sailing to the Pacific Far East.

The food, the wine, and the sour dough bread were just fabulous. We had some Army nurses along with us who added to the festive atmosphere and made our stay in San Francisco memorable.

The time eventually came when we were advised that we were to be taken to our individual states to military hospitals nearest our homes. We were happy at the thought of finally arriving home and also depressed at the though of leaving each other. Together we had watched a lot of the proverbial water pass under the bridge, torrential at times. Al Wheeler was the first to leave. *"So long, Boxie,"* followed by a strong handshake that lingered and lingered, another look at each other and without speaking, a bear-like hug followed by an almost running departure. Elmer Shabart, next, same thing. On and on till only Dan and I were left. Dear Dan, my closest companion for over three years. Slept next to each other in the boxcars, on the "hell ships," and in prison camp. Shared everything we had with each other, took care of each other when sick, and I guess we loved each other and were just finding out about it now when we were parting. We looked at each other--eyes brimming-- and reached for each other and then we were hugging each other without saying a word; we couldn't, we both were weeping. We pulled apart and said *"be seeing you,"* and each of us went his way. I was emotionally drained, devastated. How would we ever get along without each other?

The joys and sorrows I was now experiencing were getting difficult to deal with. Moments of exhilaration followed by periods of depression. It was a turmoil of emotions, expressed eloquently in some novel I had read, as

*"...like a coin with joy and sorrow etched on each face of the coin; when one face showed, the other was not visible."*

Author with children. Robert, Arnold, Donald, and Merrie. 1988.

## 41

I departed San Francisco on a hospital train along with other ex-prisoners of war from the Eastern states. After five days we arrived at Utica, N.Y., where we were taken to Rhoads General Hospital. After our assignment to various wards, we were advised that those who felt able could have seven days leave to go home.

A group of us decided to have a few drinks together before departing for home. There were five of us in the group, including an Army nurse we acquired at Rhoads Hospital. She was a cute little blonde, just home from the Pacific. So we went bar hopping! Here we were, packed, ready to return home to our families, and we go off drinking, getting more drunk by the minute. I still can't understand why we did it. I suppose, some psychologist can. Imagine, after more than four years of being away from home, and in those years thinking about nothing else but returning home, none of us wanted to go home. Whether we were timid, reluctant, frightened or suffering from some psychosis, I just don't know.

At about 11 o'clock that night I suddenly announced that I was going home. Someone said he was glad I wasn't driving--and he was right. I went to the telephone and called my mother, telling her I would arrive in New York at Grand Central Station at 6 A.M., *"and please remember, Mom, I don't want any overly emotional reception--please, Mom."* (I often thought what that poor woman must have thought at that time. She never discussed it with me.)

I fell immediately asleep on the train, as only someone can who has drunk too much. I woke up in Grand Central Terminal, walked down the platform and saw members of my family huddled together in the distance. I was carrying a bag and the Samurai Sword given to me by Lt. Hegecata. My family greeted me with cries of glee and they were all crying--Mother, Father, sisters and brothers--everyone was hugging me at the same time. I was glad I had told them to restrain their emotions or they probably would have had a band there. Suddenly, I was the one who needed emotional restraint. I just started to cry and couldn't stop. My poor family, they didn't know what to expect after my letters and phone calls home.

When I started crying, everyone else started to cry, even strangers who were watching the spectacle. My Mother's sobs, as she clung to me, shattered my low and cowardly threshold for emotional situations. My Dad grabbed me and it was the first time in my life that I saw him cry. His eyes were so full, I just couldn't cope. It wasn't over yet--my sisters and my brothers too joined in the act. It was a grand loving and crying party as the Irish would say--and they were right.

I realized that all my admonitions to them about a quiet, non-demonstrative reunion were only due to my selfishness in not wanting an emotional homecoming. Stupid me, how could it have been otherwise? I still feel badly about my actions upon returning home, but families are so great, they understand.

And Mom, the next time I become a prisoner of war, I'll let you invite the neighbors and have a band when I return.

Coming home to the old homestead was an unbelievable dream come true. I had always envisioned this "Miracle" throughout the past years and it had come to pass. Opening the iron gate, I entered the house to be greeted by all of our neighbors, friends, relatives, and old girlfriends.

They had come from all over to greet me with tears of joy and welcome that I had come home. I felt like a celebrity, but was mostly embarrassed at the plaudits heaped on me. Though it was nice too. Someone in the family had goofed and invited several of my old girlfriends to this one party. However, as a survivor I also survived this delicate situation. The party continued for several days, as distant friends and relatives came to call. I had finally and actually arrived home, returned to my family, friends, and my roots after a long delay due to causes beyond my control.

Some short time later it was Christmas and Pop and I were sitting at the base of the Christmas tree. Pop looked at me and said in a strained voice, *"The Christ Baby has brought you home to me."* I looked at him and said nothing. I wondered, how could Christ have chosen me and the others who survived over those who did not make it; most of whom I felt were more worthy of survival than I. It's a tough question to ponder and I don't know the answer. Man caused the war in his exercise of free will. God did not cause the war even though in his Omniescence he knew it would happen, and we know he grieved over all the suffering and death caused by the war. Perhaps He intervened, perhaps He didn't--we shall never know in this world.

I still didn't reply to Pop.

141

## 42

If the atomic bomb had not been dropped on Japan, I am sure I would not be writing this saga. President Harry Truman had to make the final, soul shattering decision of whether to use the bomb. It must have taken great courage. This decision has been adversely criticized by many and applauded by many. It has been termed a cruel and amoral decision. I don't think so, but if it was, someone higher up will have to make that judgement. It did, however, end a cruel war and those who steadfastly maintain that it was a wrong decision are implying that it would have been better to have allowed millions of American and Japanese servicemen to die in the planned invasion of Japan plus the many more millions of Japanese civilians who would have perished in the warfare. Do they think the Japanese would have hesitated to use the atomic bomb if they had it? As Winston Churchill said, *"The people who preferred invasion to the nuclear bomb have no intention of proceeding to the Japanese front themselves."*

War Department estimates were that one million American lives would be the expected price for the invasion of Japan. When you consider the millions of American and Japanese lives that would have been lost, all there is to say is Thank God for the atomic bomb and for President Truman's decision to use it.

The unfortunate Japanese who were killed at Hiroshima and Nagasaki were victims on the sacrificial altar of peace and everyone is saddened by the price they paid.

We have to remember that Japan infamously started the war. Before the Japanese were subdued, tamed, humiliated, and before they were given a Constitution by their American conquerors, they were in the words of Admiral Halsey, *"implacable, treacherous and barbaric."* They committed moral suicide in their cruel, sadistic and inhuman treatment of their prisoners and in doing so left a testament to their character at that time. The simple reason for dropping the bomb was to end the war--and save lives. It did, and brought peace back to a war weary world and, consequently, many Americans and Japanese have lived on to old age.

All of the prisoners of war who survived their infamous prison camps received another chance at life, actually a rebirth. Yes, war is hell, especially in a Japanese prison camp. Thank you again, Harry.

The following article, recently published, reveals the Japanese intentions regarding the lives of the prisoners under their control:

## *DOCUMENTS REVEAL JAPANESE ORDERED MASSACRE*

*Wartime documents uncovered by a Hong Kong man reveal for the first time top secret details of a Japanese World War II massacre plan. Official Japanese prisoner of war camp records discovered in October 1987 show orders calling for the massacre of all inmates of POW camps in Taiwan if the allies invaded the country as the war drew to a close.*

*The documents mysteriously disappeared at the end of the war before finally resurfacing in the U.S. National Archives in Washington, D.C. They are believed to be the only ones of their kind to have come to light since the end of*

143

*the hostilities, according to their finder, Jack Edwards.*

*Although it was widely believed the Japanese authorities had issued such orders to POW camp commanders throughout Southeast Asia, it has never been conclusively proven before. Directed to the chief of staff of the Kinkaseki POWs, the order gave explicit guidelines for the mass execution of prisoners in Taiwan camps. But the massacres were never carried out due to the sudden Japanese surrender after the explosion of the Hiroshima and Nagasaki bombs, ruling out the need for an allied invasion of Japanese occupied territories.*

EX-POW BULLETIN, May 1990

After the initial excitement of returning home had subsided, I now had a sad duty to perform; contact the families of those men whom I had known in prison camp and who were now dead. I had kept many of their addresses throughout the years of imprisonment and the others I obtained from the War Department. I visited or corresponded with all of them. They all were so eager and grateful for any word of their loved ones. It was a devastating experience at times, always overshadowed by their happiness in learning firsthand about their loved ones. Now that we know, many said, we feel so much better.

I visited the parents of the man--I should say boy-- who was among the three executed at Mukden Prison Camp for escaping. It was a difficult meeting but the happiness they expressed in seeing me, at least to learn the truth, was gratifying. There is no easy way to tell a mother and father that their son was executed by a firing squad.

I visited the family of a Navy man down in Philadelphia, PA. He had worked as a cook in the kitchen at Mukden until the accumulation of so many diseases caused

144

his death. I had visited him often while he was in the "Zero" ward (hospital) in the old Chinese camp we were first interned in at Mukden. He was pitiful, just skin and bones, lying on a straw pellet. I knew he was dying and so did he and I vowed if I ever survived, I would visit his family. His name was Leonard Deck and he died within a few days. His family, too, was so grateful for my visit and through their tears expressed their gratitude. Tough visit.

Then down to Washington, D.C. to visit the widow of Lt. Paul Mitcheller of the 17th Pursuit Squadron. To tell her he was killed on one of the prison ships after surviving for almost three years. More visits and letters to all the others on my list--Jim Philipps, Earl Hulsey, Dick Donnewald, John Crocker, Jim Murray, and on and on. Seemed like I would never get done. Mrs. Philipps, Jim's mother, came all the way to New York from Idaho just to speak with me. Jim, too, was killed on one of the "hell" ships transporting prisoners to Japan. This poor woman had also lost another son in the war. She was so sweet and understanding that she completely enveloped me in her kindness and love. We saw each other for many years after and I shall always treasure her memory.

The last ones I visited were the three children of Jim Murray, Captain of the mine planter, who was killed when our mine planter was bombed by the Japanese. I left the gory details out but still don't know if I did a good job on this one.

I tried to ease the pain for all and suspect I was also easing the pangs of the "guilt complex" which so many of us survivors had acquired.

# 43

While at home on leave from the hospital, I received notification that the U.S. government was giving all of the ex-prisoners of war a two week vacation at any resort in the United States. We were permitted to take along two guests, all expenses paid. Though in ill health, I decided to go to the Dennis Hotel in Atlantic City, NJ, taking along my mother and father. We had a grand time together. However, they expressed surprise at my apparent reluctance to discuss my prison experience. I suppose, like everyone else who had been there, I was trying to expunge the incident from my mind. I shall forever be grateful for this kind and generous gesture on the part of our government.

I spent most of the following two years in military hospitals, recuperating from the residual effects of my imprisonment, and returned to civilian life, slightly battered but not down.

Today, as I look back on this experience in my lifetime, I can say that being a prisoner of war is to experience an event that is outside the range of usual experiences for the average person; especially so when the captors' plans for treatment of their prisoners are based principally on brutality and extermination. Following are some statistics on Japanese treatment of American prisoners of war (exact figures have been impossible to establish):

Approximately 25,000 Americans captured; of these, approximately 9,700 survived.

Of the initial number, over 5,000 prisoners died while on Japanese "Hell Ships" and over 1,000 perished on the Bataan Death March alone.

These figures do not include the Filipinos and prisoners of other nationalities who died while in Japanese captivity.

The Japanese are avid baseball fans. I wonder if they know that they were "batting" over .600 in this "world series." They had great "arms" too, for bayonetting and clubbing prisoners, and "umpires" who never threw them out of the game. I hope they only "play" in their own country now.

You Japanese are a world economic power today. What you couldn't accomplish in war, you did through peaceful means, thanks to the great start obtained through the magnanimity of the Americans, your conquerors. When McArthur finished his mission in Japan in the post war years, most of you looked upon him as a deity--and rightfully so.

The occupational forces in Japan, under McArthur, even allowed your Emperor to remain as head of your nation though he was regarded as an unprosecuted war criminal by many other nations because he assumed command of all Japan's military forces in September 1941 and, obviously, approved all of Japan's actions in the war.

True, he apologized to the United States and European nations for Japan's misdeeds but he did not apologize nor offer any reparations to China and other Asian countries which his forces brutalized in their conquest. It has been estimated that many, many millions of deaths have been wrought in the name of the Emperor and Japanese Imperialism.

It is not my intention to defame your Emperor. I respect the exalted position he holds in your society as a deity, descendant of your Sun Goddess, and loved by all

Japanese. His posture after the war was dignified and exemplary. I have to conclude that he was generally misguided by his close advisors during the war years and lived to regret the actions taken in the name of imperialism.

None of us can forget Pearl Harbor, and I feel that most of the Japanese today are ashamed of it. We have some new national shrines, the bombed and sunken naval vessels containing the bodies of those men who were murdered in the Japanese sneak attack on Pearl Harbor. Murdered, yes, because no war had been declared. We also have a new day of remembrance here, December 7th, called Pearl Harbor Day or Day of Infamy, so it is difficult for us to forget. It causes many of us to wonder if we can ever completely trust you again.

Many of us resent your money invasion of our marketplace even though it is probably favorable for our economy in that we are getting some of our dollars back and your investments are aiding our businesses. We, or a lot of us, do not like the huge acquisitions you are making in our country, like our landmarks, such as Radio City, of which you presently own about 50% (would you allow us to purchase any of your landmarks?); so much of our real estate, so many of our golf courses, which you are buying up all over the United States primarily for recreational purposes of your executives living here. You have also deliberately structured your economy so as to levy prohibitive tariffs on our export goods to Japan, effectively closing the major portion of that market to imported goods.

In fairness to you, I recognize that many American firms have turned to you for financial assistance because they could not obtain needed funds from American sources. I also recognize the lead you have taken in many technologies due to your expertise in these fields, giving you world prominence for your accomplishments.

There is a "Japan-phobia" in the United States; not felt by all, but it is there--probably motivated by resentment.

It often seems ironic to me that the two greatest economic powers to emerge after World War II were Germany and Japan.

Remember, the nation that defeated you was also the nation that magnanimously rebuilt your country to a better position than it was before the war.

It has been stated that you do not teach your children in school anything about Pearl Harbor or the atrocities committed by your forces during the war. I don't blame you, I wouldn't tell my children either if I were Japanese. But you had better think about something to tell them when they are older and ask you about the American observance of Pearl Harbor day or Day of Infamy.

Our conquest of you has succeeded in making you a peaceful nation and the price was high for both of us. You have molded me to a point where I am not completely sure if I can ever wholly trust you. I am trying hard, even though my memory will be forever stained by the blood of your innocent victims who died in your prison camps.

I am surprised that you have not made some token of atonement to the families of all those men who needlessly perished in your infamous prison camps, in the form of reparations. Don't you think you owe them something? The U.S. recently granted reparations to the Japanese, despite the protests of many Americans, including most ex-prisoners of war, who objected to the payment of $20,000 to Japanese interned in the U.S. I feel that any Japanese who were interned and suffered damages to their property because it was not properly safeguarded by U.S. authorities should be compensated for any actual proven damages sustained, in the amount of the damages only.

In retrospect, we can say today that it was unfair to intern Japanese living in the United States simply because they were of Japanese origin, and that they were unjustly interned. However, I feel that the decision was reasonable and proper <u>at that time</u>. The perfidy and treacherousness

149

of the Japanese was manifested by their sneaky, unfair and deceptive attack on Pearl Harbor. The wanton bombing of a nation that was not at war with them. The interests of our national security, further aggravated by the severe losses inflicted on lives and property in Hawaii, left few other options for consideration. The Japanese posture for honor and integrity was destroyed because the bombing of Pearl Harbor was effected while the Japanese Ambassador was in conference with the U.S. State Department about peace proposals until the day before Pearl Harbor was attacked. (And you don't travel from Japan to Pearl Harbor in one day!). Further, in early 1942, the Dies Commission in Washington, D.C. published a 285 page report on Japanese espionage activities against the U.S., including plans, charts, codes, maps and details concerning the hypothetical invasion of the U.S. The Commission also called special attention to Japanese infiltration into local governments.

The internment of enemy aliens is standard procedure for any nation at war and any person who is not a citizen of this country is an alien.

There has never been any instance of mistreatment or brutality recorded against any Japanese interned in this country. At the time of the internment, we had no way to determine which of the Japanese living in this country were loyal Americans, hence the ruling to intern them.

Americans of Japanese descent, later on in the war, admirably proved their loyalty, courage and their Americanism by distinguishing themselves in the European Theatre of War where their fierce fighting earned them more decorations for valor than any other units fighting in the area.

I salute and respect each one of them as true patriots and can only say to them that I wish there were some other more favorable alternative available at the time of the internment of those Japanese living in America.

The argument has been put forth that if we interned

the Japanese living here, why didn't we intern people of other nationalities whose countries we were also at war with? I don't know the answer to that, except to say that their countries did not insidiously bomb us before war was declared.

As far as reparations go, it appears to me that if any reparations are considered, it should be on the part of the Japanese government to all the prisoner of war families, of all nationalities, who perished in their infamous prison camps.

I hope you never become a world military power again as I am still a little uneasy about the inherent characteristics you exhibited while striving to become a military power in WWII. You have obviously changed now. Why not? Your former enemy revived you without using Bushido; our Armed Forces are protecting you, and we are paying for it; you are prosperous, much more prosperous than some of the nations that defeated you; and you know, you have won WWIII without firing a shot--through peaceful means. I wonder what Tojo and his gang would say if they were around today.

I hope that your success will serve as an example to other nations with warlike ambitions. I also hope that there is nothing sinister lurking behind the benign facade you now exhibit; behind the toothy smile; behind the friendly hiss; behind the handshake you now extend instead of bowing from the waist; and behind your generally benevolent posture. I must admit, I don't think there is.

# 44

Those of us who survived the agony and despair of Bataan and Corregidor and who further survived 3 1/2 years of living hell in Japan prison camps; who endured danger, cruelty, beatings, misery, sickness, and starvation will never really be whole again. It is a humbling and despairing experience to learn that your precious life is of such small value to your captors. I neglected to mention one of the most common diseases most of us acquired--hate--which you, our captors, transmitted to us. Fortunately, there is a cure, but the medicine takes a long, long time to work. In addition to the scars many of us bear from battle wounds, we also have emotional scars which, unlike battle scars, will never heal but remain a reminder for the rest of our lives.

I often feel, as someone suggested, that we are "damaged goods." The memories are constantly recalled with great emotional impact. Sometimes with intent, oftentimes without. Sometimes an inner rage sets in, sometimes deep depression. As I have mentioned, so many of us have a peculiar subconscious guilt complex over having survived; a kind of feeling of breaking trust with our dead companions--why were we so much luckier than they?

It has also been said that understanding comes to each of us through the pathways of our own experiences. I trod one pathway for more than three years and while I understand a lot of what happened, there is still an awful lot I don't understand.

Being a prisoner of war taught me values I was not previously conscious of. Values like patience, thrift (not in the monetary sense, but in things like water and food), discipline, self-suffering, suffering for others, fierce loyalty, fairness and love of my fellow man. The greatest revelation to me was the loss of freedom, a value which most of us Americans take for granted. Unfortunately, we only learn how precious it is when it is taken away from us and our lives and freedom are at the whim and command of an aggressor. The price of freedom is high, but worth fighting for--which is perhaps the greatest lesson I learned in this experience.

I repeat, if you wish to enjoy the benefits offered in this great land of ours, then you must share in the responsibilities.

The experience was rich in learning about my fellow man, with hate and--paradoxically--love scenting our surroundings. I have no personal bitterness for the experience fate dealt me. I feel it would be selfish, because someone had to be there in the position I was in; and to wish that I had not been there would only imply that I wished someone else there in my place. I couldn't do that to anyone. I just "went" where I was "sent," as did millions of men and women serving in the Armed Forces, performing whatever task was assigned to us, wherever we were sent. If there were any heroes, they all were.

It was a saga of man's inhumanity to man, of cruelty, of man's humanity to man, of love and hatred. The lesson learned is that all people must learn to substitute love for hate. Hate is an obnoxious four-letter-word, never to be used except to hate "HATE."

There is nothing new or revealing in these words, as I am merely repeating what we all know and what a famous man said over two thousand years ago--*"love one another as I love you"*--and He sure knew what He was talking about.

To my fallen comrades who did not come home, I

say, you are not forsaken, nor forgotten, and you will always live on in memories of love and affection. You are the true heroes of this episode in history, you are the men who gave up your tomorrows so we could have our todays. Your vision, gaunt and emaciated as it was, will always be carried in mind and heart as pure beauty shining forth like a bright beacon in darkness--a beacon of love.

You have answered your country's call, serving with honor, distinction, and your lives.

Letter to St. Peter

*Let them in, Peter, they are very tired,*
*Give them couches where the Angels sleep.*
*Let them wake whole again*
*To new dawns fired,*
*With sun, not war. And may their peace be deep;*
*Remember where the broken bodies lie,*
*And give them things they like, let them make noise,*
*God knows how young they were to die!*
*Give swing bands, not gold harps, to these our boys.*
*Let them love, Peter, they have had no time.*
*Girls sweet as meadow winds with flowing hair.*
*They should have trees and bird songs, hills to climb,*
*The taste of summer in a ripened pear. Tell them*
*How they are missed. Say not to fear.*
*It's going to be alright*
*With us down here.*

Elma Dean

It is always nice to tell a story with a happy ending. This one has one too; some of us survived, we learned a lot, we are proud to be Americans, proud to have served, proud to be called patriots; and proud to have the Stars and Stripes flying over us again. We learned the value of freedom and that our Democracy and way of life are the best in this world. We always knew, but learned again:

## "IT'S A GRAND OLD FLAG"

by Louis Panagini

# EPILOGUE

If you are surprised that the person who wrote this narrative is still alive today, more than 45 years after these events, so am I.

I look forward eagerly each year to our annual reunion of "The Defenders of Bataan and Corregidor," which is held in a different locale every year. Our ranks have thinned markedly throughout the years. Those of us still surviving enjoy a very special kind of comradeship with each other; affection, respect, and I guess, love.

We don't drink as much as we used to; some of us have even stopped smoking. A lot of us are widowers. We sit around a lot, have a few drinks and reminisce about our days together. Most of us go to bed by 10 P.M. A great sense of serenity permeates the atmosphere because we are with each other again and understand each other's feelings and thoughts--we are a family.

So very many have died since returning home. We talk about them at times, over and over again--there will always be a special place for them in our hearts.

*War Generation*
*We, whom the storm winds battered, come again*
*Like strangers to the places we have known.*
*Who sought man's understanding, all in vain,*
*For hardened hearts to grief's dark image grown.*
*So, passing through the careless crowd alone,*
*Ghosts of a time no future can restore,*
*We desolately roam forever more*

*An empty shore*
*For us they live till life itself shall end.*
*The frailties and the follies of those years,*
*Their strength which only pride of loss could*
*lend.*
*Their vanished hopes, their sorrows and their*
*tears;*
*But slowly towards the verge, the dim sky clears.*
*For nobler men may yet redeem our clay,*
*When we and war together, one wise day*
*Have passed away.*

Vera Brittain, 1914

Some years ago I read a book by a survivor of the Nazi Holocaust. I regret I neither recall the name of the book nor the author's name. However, it was an account of his incarceration in a Nazi concentration camp and revealed that he was forced to watch the murder of his wife and children by their captors.

After his initial horror and grief, he said that he realized the deaths of his loved ones were caused by hatred, and the only thing that could prevent a recurrence of this carnage, was love. He had to substitute love for hate, and he did it. He taught himself to love those people who had murdered his family. Hatred breeds hatred, he said, and the only hope for this universe is to love one another.

Tough act to follow.

I do not hate any Japanese in this world of today. Japan is now a democracy and a different country. I have forgiven those Japanese of World War II against whom my bitterness had been directed; but loving them is still very difficult for me--though I will keep trying.

157

Author, with family, after presentation of Prisoner of War Medal by Congressman G. Hochbrueckner at Town Hall, Southhold, NY. 1988.
Photo by J. Maclellan